World Money
世界货币

（英）格里·贝利 费利西娅·劳 ◎著
（英）马克·比奇 ◎插图
傅瑞蓉 ◎译

目录 Contents

4～5　谁需要钱？
我们所有人都需要钱，没有钱，整个世界都将陷入瘫痪。

6～7　货币已经有6 000年的历史了
货币的历史非常悠久。

8～11　飘洋过海
随着国际贸易的发展，货币也变得国际化了。

12～17　世界货币
今天，世界各国的货币千差万别。

18～19　货币兑换
当我们想把一个国家的货币兑换为另一个国家的货币时，该怎么做？

20～31　贸易
随着货物的飘洋过海，货币也随时在交换或兑换。

32～35　制定价格
货币也能像其他商品一样进行买卖。

36～41　银行业务
世界各地的银行买卖不同国家的货币，并让货币流通起来。

42～45　世界财富
最富裕的国家都是在经济上取得成功的国家，它们生产和出口很多商品并不断增长。

46～47 **世界贫困**
贫穷的国家往往要承受各种各样的困难，它们需要有助于它们贸易发展和经济繁荣的外力援助。

48～55 **让世界更平等**
一些世界性的组织和小型贸易商是如何促成富国和穷国之间开展贸易并共同促进的？

56～57 **快乐的财富**
金钱并不一定能带来快乐。那么，一个国家该如何评价自己的经济表现呢？

58～59 **联合的世界**
世界还不太平，但是世界各国相互帮助的途径非常多。所有人都通过贸易和相互交往联系在了一起，你也是"链条"中的一环。

60～61 **中英文术语对照表**

62～63 **索引**

64 **译后记**

附 英文影印版

谁需要钱?

世界上每个人都要用钱。钱的正式名称是"货币"。在不同的国家，货币的样子看上去各不相同，它们有不同的名称，也有完全不一样的价值，但是无论如何，它们都发挥着"钱"的作用。这是因为，世界各国的政府决定了什么样的钱是可以合法使用的。

大家一致认可

每一个使用钱的人（我们知道，每个人都要用钱，因此这也就等于说世界上每一个人）全都同意，货币是这样一种东西：

* 它是计量财富总值的单位。
* 你可以用它来换取东西，或者你可以用它来进行买卖。
* 它也可以作为一种商品，你可以像买卖咖啡一样地买卖美元和英镑。
* 你可以用它来奖励员工，也可以把它当做礼物送人。总之，你可以用它做你想做的任何事情。

但是，所有人都承认，它是有价值的。

日复一日，货币的价值变还是不变？

买东西的时候，每个人都同意他们的货币的价值。一般来说，日复一日，每一枚硬币或每一张纸币的价值，或者说购买力，并不会出现太大的变化。一美元就是一美元，不管是今天还是明天，它都能购买到差不多相同数量的东西（尽管可能稍有差别）。

当然，如果一个国家突然发生了非常重大的事件，比如说战争，那么，硬币和纸币的价值就有可能会突然改变。在发生这种事件的时候，有可能会出现食物匮乏的情况，这时，你购买一袋大米或许就不得不使用比以前更多的钱了。而且要记住，在没有发生灾难的时候，也可能会出现这种情况。

相信钱

因此，每个国家都有自己的货币。每个生活在其中的人都相信它、使用它并接受它，都认为它具有一定的价值。但是，我们也相信其他国家的钱吗？并且也会毫不犹豫地使用其他国家的钱吗？为什么我们需要使用其他国家的钱呢？

也许我们与另一个国家之间相距千万公里，但是，就贸易而言，当我们购买其他国家的商品时，一般都需要用其他国家的货币来进行支付。

实际上，所有的货币都是世界货币。

货币已经有6 000年的历史了

世界上的各种货币并没有什么新奇独特之处，这是因为贸易并不是什么新生事物。国与国之间进行贸易往来已经有好几千年的历史了，也就是说，随着商人的四处走动以及货物的买卖，各个国家之间不断地发生着货币的交换。

物物交换

大家都知道，当两个人都想得到对方手中的东西时，毫无疑问，物物交换或者以货易货是一个好方法。这丝毫不足为奇。真正令人惊讶的是，物物交换持续了那么长时间，而且还出现在了那么多个不同的社会中。

在人类社会的早期，当我们的祖先在一个地方定居下来并在那里种植庄稼的时候，他们通常都会发现，有太多东西需要种植了，同时他们拥有的东西又太少了。他们需要拿剩余的产品去交换，以换回他们需要的东西。这就意味着将会出现市场，也意味着将会产生交易。

最早的交易是物与物之间的交换。当然，买卖双方要想就他们各自拥有的商品的价值达成一致意见，并确定双方都想要对方的商品，并不是一件很容易的事情。

超越村落范围

起初,是一个村落或部落的人与另一个村落或部落的人进行物物交换。随着时间的推移,无论是必需品(例如钵、盆和织物等),还是奢侈品(例如珠宝和葡萄酒等),它们的交易都变得越来越频繁了,同时商人们的活动范围也变得越来越大,他们会长途跋涉到更远的地方去交换货物。随着交易量的不断增长,物物交换的形式也就变得越来越复杂了,人们需要一种更好的交易方式。

硬币的出现

物物交换的发展最终导致了硬币的出现,它是"交换的媒介"。后来,同样充当"交换的媒介"的纸币也出现了。而这就意味着,大家已经普遍接受了货币是货物的替代品,并且货币自身就是有价值的。换句话说,现在货物可以与货币进行"交换"了,或者说,可以用货币去交换货物了。

硬币的安抚作用

然而,在被当做"交换的媒介"之前,硬币就已经被使用了很长的一段时间。最初,硬币并不是用来交易的,而是用来安抚敌人的。英语中的动词"pay(支付)"源于拉丁语中的"pacare(给付)"这个单词,它的原意是"安抚"或者"讲和"。

如果一个部

落想与另一个部落讲和,那么,它就会支付给另一个部落一些双方都能接受的"有价值的东西",这样,这两个部落就能够实现和平。

早期的硬币的作用就在于此。

飘洋过海

就在几百年前,世界贸易打开了各个国家的大门。现在,商人们穿越重洋,跨越大洲,开辟了一条条贸易线路,它们纵横交错,通往全世界的每一个角落。国与国之间的贸易进一步扩大了。

新兴的商人

在整个16世纪和17世纪,陆上和海上贸易都得到了极大的发展,涌现出了许多新的大港口,围绕这些港口的地方后来都发展成了繁华的商业中心。

随着对外贸易的发展,出现了一大批商人和探险者,他们用本国的商品换了许多本国没有的稀有物品,然后再把这些物品卖给本国的富人——当然,这些富人以前可能从来没有见到过这些东西。通过这种方法,这些商人自己也变得富裕起来了。

来来往往

1271年,马可·波罗跟随他的父亲和叔叔离开了意大利的威尼斯,一路向东旅行,最后到达了中国。中国当时恰好是元朝,在伟大的忽必烈的统治之下。他们是穿过古代的"丝绸之路"到达中国的,并且在中国待了整整24年。马可·波罗证明了与遥远的国家进行贸易是可能的,也是有利可图的。

随后,欧洲的航海探险家,比如哥伦布、瓦斯科·达·伽马和麦哲伦,开始向东航行,然后再折向西方,发现了新的大陆和新的交易机会。

差不多在同一个时期,中国的郑和也携带着一些最基本的航海图、地图和航海设备,向相反的方向行进,即由东向西航行。他的船队是当时有史以来最庞大的船队。

对外贸易

他们都希望能够发现新的富裕的国家,他们可以在那些国家里搜集各种极具异国情调的产品——从烟草、橄榄油、香料到黄金、玻璃制品和珍禽异兽(如猴子)。

销售的商品

国外的食品

油和香料

珍禽异兽

黄金和贵重的珠宝

所有这些商品都是新奇而令人激动的,人们很乐意把它们带回家。

繁忙的海洋

人们很容易想当然地认为，我们买到的丝绸服装都产自于中国和泰国，我们喝的茶叶都来自于印度，葡萄都是从西班牙空运来的，小朋友的爸爸们开的汽车都是日本制造的。今天，国际贸易对我们来讲，实在太熟悉了。

巨大的贸易港口

随着贸易的增长，发展出了许多巨大的国际港口。新加坡成了东西方贸易的枢纽。许多欧洲的港口，比如意大利的热那亚、葡萄牙的里斯本、英国的伦敦，成了航海探险的出发地。当然，这些地方也成了贸易和商业的中心。

今天，几乎每一个拥有海岸线或者拥有与海相通的大型河流的国家，都拥有一些大型的港口。

集装箱运输

现在,世界各国的大部分货物都是先装进集装箱,然后通过海轮运往世界各国去的。集装箱里的货物可以随意堆放,它更方便运输货物。我们可以把集装箱装满货物之后再装上轮船、卡车和火车,而且装卸集装箱也很容易。

全世界的大港口

中国的上海港
新加坡的新加坡港
中国的香港
韩国的釜山港
阿拉伯联合酋长国
　(阿联酋)的迪拜港
荷兰的鹿特丹港
中国台湾地区的高雄港
德国的汉堡港
美国的洛杉矶港

钱是把我们联系在一起的纽带

如果没有钱,现代贸易就不可能发生。因此,是钱把我们联系在了一起。工作、消费、储蓄、旅游……全都与钱有关。其实,钱把你和千千万万个其他人联系在了一起,其中有许多是你完全陌生的人。所有这些人都影响着你的生活!

下面,就让我们来看个究竟:钱到底是什么东西?

世界货币

事实是，货币并不是某一个特定的国家发明出来的。在全世界的许多国家和地区，都曾出现过货币，这些货币都有自己的演变过程。当某种货币出现后，随着它在不同国家之间的交流和传递，它的形式也在不断地发生着变化。

鼓　贝壳　羽毛　珠子

早期的罗马硬币上印着罗穆卢斯（Romulus）和雷穆斯（Remus）的头像，他们是孪生兄弟，罗马国的创立者

来自希腊和中国（原文此处误为日本。——译者）的两枚非常古老的硬币

小玩意儿

在过去，各种各样让你意想不到的小东西，都曾经被人们拿来当钱使用过——琥珀、珠子、贝壳、鼓、蛋、羽毛等，不胜枚举。

有价值的硬币

后来，在世界各地，小块的银和金充当了一般等价物，只不过有些地方早一些，有些地方晚一些而已。这些贵重的金属之所以被选中，是因为它们本身就是有价值的。它们能够充当衡量价值的标准尺度，由此每个人都知道一头牛或一只鸭子到底值多少金币。

纸币

纸币始于欧洲，它最早其实是人们把黄金存入金匠的金库时的收据。这种收据事实上是一个承诺，它承诺在该收据被它的所有者出示时，金匠必须支付一定金额的黄金。很快地，这些收据本身也就变成了一种货币，即纸币。直到今天，我们还在使用纸币。

各国的纸币从上到下依次为：
尼泊尔
马来西亚
埃及
美国
欧洲
中国

与"钱"有关的一些词汇

货币
被大家所普遍接受的钱的形式，包括纸币和硬币，由各国政府发行。

面值
硬币种类很多，比如说欧元、瑞士法郎和澳元等，全世界有几百种不同的硬币。硬币和纸币上清楚地印着它们的价值，这就是所谓的面值。

票面价值
票面价值通常指的是，印刷在纸币和硬币上面的、人们一般会相信的货币的价值。

法定货币
法定货币指的是，被一个国家政府所采纳的通行的各种货币，在它们上面印有各种不同的面值。

你自己的钱

以下列举了世界上一些国家和地区的货币,以及它们特殊的名称。

阿富汗

阿尔及利亚

澳大利亚

不丹

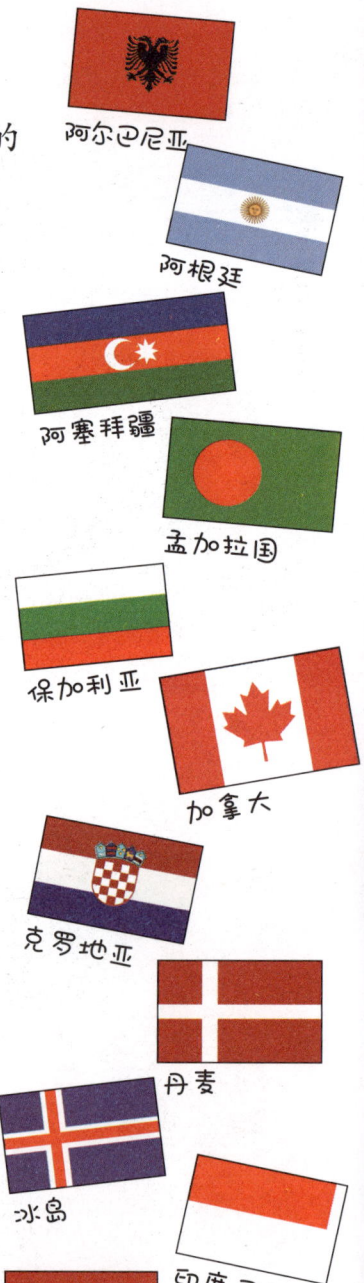

阿富汗	阿富汗尼
阿尔巴尼亚	阿尔巴尼亚列克
阿尔及利亚	阿尔及利亚第纳尔
阿根廷	阿根廷比索
澳大利亚	澳大利亚元
阿塞拜疆	阿塞拜疆马纳特
孟加拉国	孟加拉塔卡
不丹	不丹努扎姆
巴西	巴西雷亚尔
保加利亚	保加利亚列弗
加拿大	加拿大元
智利	智利比索
中国	人民币
克罗地亚	克罗地亚库纳
捷克共和国	捷克克朗
丹麦	丹麦克朗
埃及	埃及镑
匈牙利	匈牙利福林
冰岛	冰岛克朗
印度	印度卢比
印度尼西亚	印度尼西亚盾

巴西

智利 中国

捷克

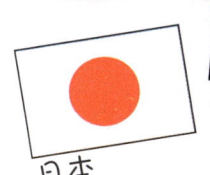
日本

伊拉克

韩国

伊朗

南非

马来西亚

新西兰

摩洛哥

巴基斯坦

挪威

秘鲁

罗马尼亚

菲律宾

俄罗斯

伊朗	伊朗里亚尔
伊拉克	伊拉克第纳尔
日本	日元
韩国	韩元
马来西亚	马来西亚林吉特
墨西哥	墨西哥比索
摩洛哥	摩洛哥迪拉姆
新西兰	新西兰元
挪威	挪威克朗
巴基斯坦	巴基斯坦卢比
秘鲁	秘鲁新索尔
菲律宾	菲律宾比索
罗马尼亚	罗马尼亚列伊
俄罗斯	俄罗斯卢布
沙特阿拉伯	沙特阿拉伯里亚尔
南非	南非兰特
瑞典	瑞典克朗
瑞士	瑞士法郎
泰国	泰铢
土耳其	土耳其里拉
乌克兰	乌克兰格里夫纳
英国	英镑
美国	美元
越南	越南盾

瑞士

沙特阿拉伯

土耳其

泰国
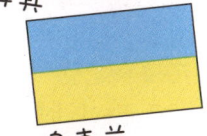
乌克兰

美国

英国

越南

外　币

如果世界上所有的国家都使用同一种纸币和硬币，那么，这个世界肯定会变得简单很多。如果真是那样，那么，我们所有人都将使用同一种"世界泰勒（worldthalar）"，就像某些早期的科幻作家所描述的那样。但是，我们知道，几乎每个国家都有它自己的货币，即使这些货币都叫同一个名称，并且也有相同的货币单位，比如说元、分，但也并不意味着它们的实际价值是相同的。

购买货币

如果你打算到国外去度假，那么，你就需要购买外国货币。举例来说，如果你打算去法国，那么，你就需要欧元；如果你打算去美国，那么，你就需要美元；如果你打算去中国，那么，你就需要人民币。

你可以向银行购买外币——大多数银行都有外汇柜台，甚至邮局也有，只要你想要的外币不是太不寻常的就不会有问题。在邮局里，你可能无法兑换到阿尔巴尼亚列克或哥伦比亚比索，但是兑换欧元、美元和英镑是没有问题的。在换汇时，每一个出售外币的机构都会向你收取一定的费用，这项费用是按你所兑换的总价值的百分比来计算的，每笔业务只收取少量的费用。

外国货币

当你碰到别的国家发行的硬币和纸币时，会怎么样呢？它还是钱吗？是的，它当然是钱。因为你可以用它在发行它的国家里买东西，也可以用它去购买其他国家的货币。

举个例子来说，如果你拿到了日元，你可以用它来购买英镑或美元或其他货币。这就是所谓的货币兑换。

外汇交易行情表上显示的是世界上主要货币的买进和卖出价格

汇率

在兑换外汇时，由于汇率不一样，你在银行（或者在网上）兑换往往要比在大街上的外汇处兑换更加合算。不过，请你注意，购买外汇和卖出外汇时的汇率是不一样的。当你购买外汇时，你总能获得一个更好的汇率，因为货币兑换商通常会给出两个汇率。不过，在你回国之前，你最好把你所有的外币都花出去。

你通常能够在当地的兑换处以相当合算的汇率兑换货币

17

货币兑换

当国与国之间进行贸易时,大多数国家都想使用本国的货币来做买卖。因此,在发生国际贸易之前,有可能会发生货币贸易。举例来说,如果你想从中国购买一些灯笼,那你就必须用中国的人民币进行支付。这就意味着你得先用你自己国家的英镑或美元或比索去购买人民币。

使用美元

目前,许多国家都把它们本国货币的价值与美元的价值挂钩,这样事情就变得简单了。这就是所谓的固定汇率制度。那么,这种制度是怎么运行的呢?

每个国家决定多少本国货币才值1美元呢?它大致是这样的:1元人民币=0.16美元。这意味着,你将需要用6元多的人民币才能买到1美元。

如果你给中国的供货商1美元的话,那你就会得到6只灯笼和一些零钱。

有时候,如果双方都同意使用某一种货币(比如说美元)时,贸易就会变得更加容易了。因此,假设1只中国灯笼的价值为1元人民币,那么,

浮动汇率

有些货币的汇率是可以自由"浮动"的。这个意思是，货币的汇率每天都会有所变化。货币的价值取决于市场供求关系。有些货币很受欢迎，人们愿意购买和投资它们，它们的价值就高；有些货币不太受人欢迎，它们的价值就会较低。

买入和卖出货币

汇率每天都会被公示出来，世界各国的人都能看到。银行和货币兑换商（其实是每个与货币有切身关系的人）都会仔细地研究各种货币的汇率，以保证自己能够以合适的汇率来兑换他们自己需要的货币。

货币的买卖与货物的买卖是一样的，比如说跟小麦和石油的买卖一样。货币贸易商在做买卖时也需要时刻提高警惕，因为汇率分分钟都在发生变化。

如果你在早上的时候买进了1 000美元，也许在下午时它有可能值更多钱了。

贸 易

大多数国家用它们所赚到的钱做的事情都与买卖有关,而买和卖则与贸易有关——人们用钱购买他们所需要的东西,并且也把东西卖给有需要的人。贸易让货币流通了起来。

贸易——协议

因为贸易涉及货物的交换,也就是让买卖双方都感到满意的交换。贸易总是涉及协议或合同,交易一旦完成就不可更改;你履约了,你便完成了一笔交易,这样这笔交易也就结束了。这就是交易的全部。

专业化

几千年前,当人们第一次在村庄定居下来并且开始了农耕生活之后,便通过与其他村庄进行交换的方式来处理他们多余的产品。与此同时,一些村庄开始在某些事情上比别的村庄做得更快、更好,比如说在制作箭头、猛犸象吊坠上。这就是所谓的专业化,它创造了更大的贸易需求。

国际贸易

同样的道理也适用于今天，只不过今天专业化的生产规模更大而已。一些国家或者民族地区往往专注于制造和提供与其他国家相比，具有天然优势的产品和服务。

假设这个世界上只有两个国家：沙特阿拉伯和牙买加。沙特阿拉伯盛产石油，它生产出来的石油远远超出了本国的需要，但是这个国家的土地却无法种植甘蔗，而沙特阿拉伯的每个人都想要红糖；牙买加因为气候适宜，它适合种植大量的甘蔗，但是它却需要进口石油来提炼汽油和取暖的燃料等。

再假设沙特阿拉伯与牙买加之间的贸易不存在任何障碍，那么，沙特阿拉伯就可以向牙买加出口石油，而牙买加则可以向沙特阿拉伯出口红糖。它们可以相互交换两国各自拥有的最有优势的商品。

夜晚灯火通明的炼油厂

牙买加的甘蔗种植园

这种专业化的贸易允许某个国家出售商品以赚取金钱，从而购买它自己无法种植的产品和不能生产的原料及其产品。

这就是所谓的国际贸易。

进出口

相互购买

向国外购进商品和服务在国内销售，这被称为进口。进口需要花费进口国的钱，因为进口公司需要为这些货物和服务付款。因此，钱是由国内向国外流出的。

国家之所以要进口某些商品和服务，是因为这些商品和服务是必需的，但是本国又无法把它们生产出来，或者也可能是因为从国外购买比在自己国家制造更加便宜。

配额

大部分进口都会有一些限制条件，比如说进口税，通常也把它称为"关税"。在通常情况下，只能进口一定数量的商品，这就是所谓的配额。

比方说，在你自己的国家，有很多工人通过制造汽车谋生。如果你的国家允许进口大量的更便宜的外国汽车，那么能够卖出去的当地汽车会更少，汽车工人就会失业。因此，有时候这种保护是必要的。

相互销售

出口是指本国提供商品和服务供其他国家的公司和政府购买。出口或大量向国外出售商品，对一个国家是有利的，因为它能为一个国家带来现金并创造财富。

通过出口赚得的钱有利于增加一个国家的财富。出口通常是按照供应商的货币支付的。这些出口的货物和服务都是出口国很容易生产出来的，而又都是国外所想要的。

比如说，美国之所以出口耐克鞋，是因为它很受欢迎，而不是因为进口耐克鞋的国家需要它。同时，美国有大片大片的土地都非常适合种植小麦，因此，美国通常出口小麦到那些无法自己种植小麦的国家。

易趣（eBay）

易趣是世界各国的人用来完成交易的许许多多个新平台之一。通过易趣，交易双方就不需要相互碰面了——他们在网上进行交易。

易趣是世界上最大的在线交易市场。试着想象一下，这是一个超过1亿个人在做买卖的大市场！在一定程度上，它就像一个当地的街头市场，只不过它存在于网络空间而已。在这个全球性的拍卖网站上，人们不仅可以相互买卖东西，还可以进行聊天、讨价还价，就像是数百年前的古老的集市一样。

易趣上有许多职业卖家，而且与这些职业卖家一样，还有数以百万计的人，他们通过在易趣上销售东西而增加自己的收入。

保持贸易平衡

有时候,你会听到某个新闻播报员说,你们国家的贸易出现了盈余(出超)或赤字(入超)。他们会报出一个数百万英镑或者几十亿英镑的数字。你可能想知道,做这些贸易的到底是哪些人?为什么要用那么多的钱?现在让我告诉你吧,它没你想象得那么复杂。

保持平衡

一个国家的贸易平衡与这个国家向国外出售的东西和从国外购进的东西有关。

大多数国家都试图在进口和出口之间找到平衡,因此,当它们向国外出口大量货物的时候,也会同时进口大量的货物。

总之,流进和流出一个国家的货币是这个国家的经济的组成部分。

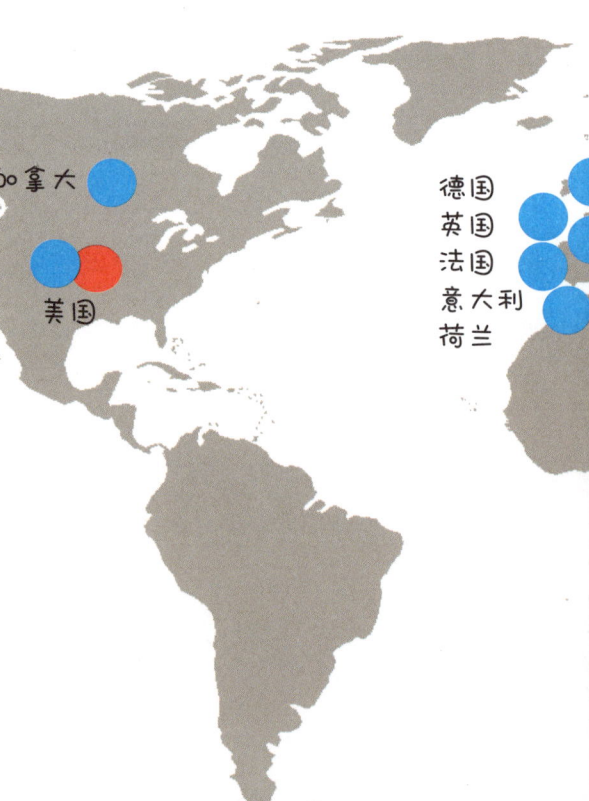

贸易差额

一个国家的出口与进口之间的差额叫作贸易差额。进口与出口相当叫作贸易平衡。

国际收支平衡表

国际收支平衡表被各国政府用来记录它们国家资金的流动情况。一个国家有了国际收支平衡表，它就能够确知进出口之间的经常项目差额是否可以接受，或者是否需要采取某种措施来实现平衡。每个国家每年都要编制国际收支平衡表。

世界上最大的进口国及地区
* 美国
* 德国
* 英国
* 法国
* 日本
* 中国
* 意大利
* 加拿大
* 中国香港
* 荷兰

世界上最大的出口国
* 中国
* 美国
* 德国
* 日本
* 法国
* 韩国
* 荷兰
* 俄罗斯
* 意大利
* 英国

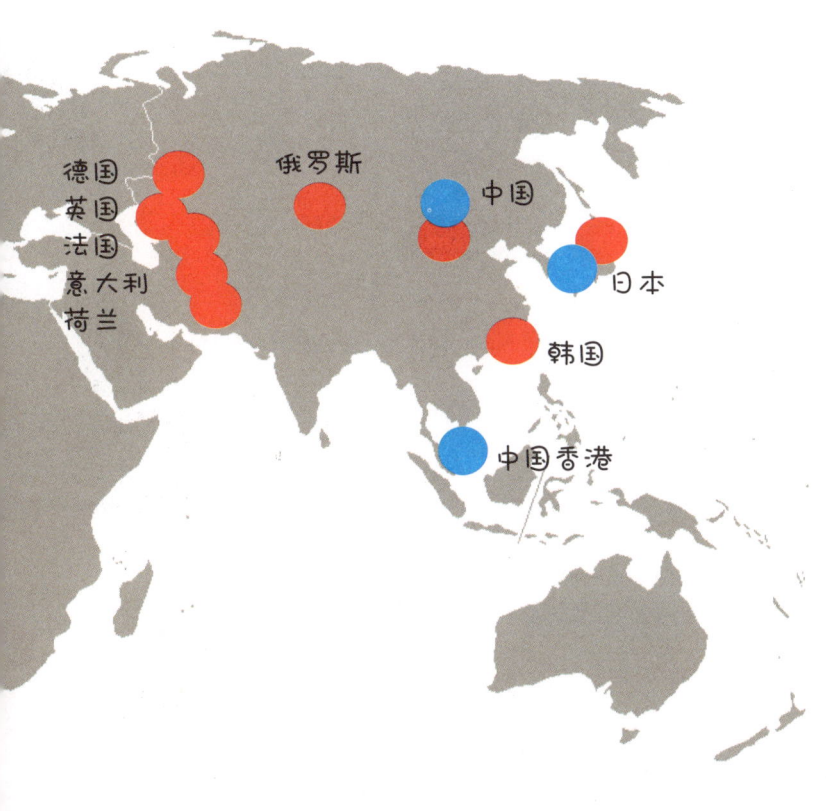

各个国家都在卖些什么东西？

世界上的大部分货物都由以下 10 个国家所出售，那么，它们都在卖些什么呢？

| 中国 | 电力机械，数据处理设备  |

| 德国  | 机动车辆，机械，化工，纺织品，交通运输设备，食品  |

| 美国 | 工业用品和材料，食品  |

| 日本 | 汽车  半导体  |

| 法国 | 农产品  机械，车辆 |

| 韩国 | 半导体，电信设备  |

| 荷兰 | 机械设备，化学品，燃料  |

| 意大利 |  纺织品和服装，生产设备 |

| 俄罗斯 | 石油和其他石油产品  |

| 英国 | 制成品，化工产品，食品 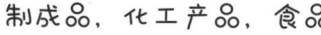 |

 服装，纺织品，铁，钢　　　　光学和医疗设备

计算机和电子产品，电气设备，
橡胶和塑料制品　　　　医药，金属

 汽车，消费品，燃料和石油产品　　　　动物饲料，饮料，飞机　

钢铁　　汽车零部件，塑料原料和发电机械

飞机　塑料，化学品，饮料　　药品，铁，钢，电子产品

　汽车，计算机，钢　　船舶和石油化工产品

食品

　汽车，化工产品，食品　饮料

机械产品，运输设备，矿产品和有色金属

天然气，金属，木材，其他木制品，化工产品，军事装备和武器

饮料

27

世界品牌

一个品牌可以是一个产品，也可以是一组产品或者一个公司，但是它不止于此。它是一个名字、一种联想。当你想起某个产品或者某一组产品时，它早已深深印入你的脑海之中了。它们往往是非常宝贵的资产，因为人们愿意为某一公司的强势品牌产品支付更多的钱。

世界品牌

"可口可乐"可能是全世界最为人们所熟知的品牌了。也就是说，当你想到一种褐色的、甜甜的、让你觉得非常好喝的碳酸饮料时，跳入你脑海中的第一个词便是"可口可乐"。"耐克"是另一个会让人们马上就认出来的品牌。

一个品牌同时也是一种承诺。几乎所有知名品牌的拥有者都会努力创建并维系一整套消费者喜欢和理解的价值观。他们都希望自己的品牌代表着某种值得信赖的、诚实的东西。

苹果公司因它的计算机和软件而闻名于世

麦当劳是一个备受人们喜爱的饮食店品牌

可口可乐是一种世界性的饮料

耐克公司的商店遍布全球各个角落

顶级品牌

每年许多人都会被问及他们心目中最好的品牌是哪些。有意思的是，在美国，大多数顶级品牌都已经融入美国人的生活当中了。所有以下这些品牌你可能都认得出来：

盖普	苹果
迪士尼	耐克
麦当劳	可口可乐
肯德基	星巴克

29

海 关

由于今天我们生活在一个高科技的世界当中,因此,在国际贸易中,国与国之间的大部分买卖都是利用汇票,通过电话、互联网和银行来完成的。

汇票

如果在买卖中使用汇票,那么,当某一位贸易商决定支付一定金额给另一位贸易商时,他就可以要求银行来进行支付。汇票里面会标明需要支付的金额以及支付的日期。

税收和关税

一旦货物被送达码头或机场,它们就会被装进某一个仓库里储存起来,直到它们通过海关的检验为止。

这是为什么呢?因为各国政府都可以从国际贸易中赚钱。政府通过向这些进口货物征收一种叫作"关税"的税收而赚钱。

不管你信不信,关税也可以作为一种对抗另一国的武器。如果A国基于某种原因想制裁B国,它就可以运用高额关税对B国的进口商品征收高额关税,这样,B国便不可能再以合理的价格出售商品,它的出口贸易就会受到损害。

缴纳关税

每次你出国旅游以及旅游回国时,你都会通过海关。在海关,你有可能会被拦下来接受检查。

海关人员会检查你的行李,以确保在你的行李里没有携带什么需要支付关税或其他税收的东西。你被允许携带一定数量的免税商品。但是如相机、手表之类的物品,可能就要纳税了。

你最好对你所携带的物品先进行报关;如果不报关,那你就违法了,到时候海关对你的罚款会让你花掉更多的钱。

要缴纳哪些税

关税

海关人员的职责有两个:一是检查过境货物;二是征收合理的关税。关税类型主要有两种——

从量税 它是按照货物的数量来征收的,比如说规定一桶石油收多少税,而与一桶石油的具体价值无关。

从价税 它是按照货物总价值的百分比来征收的。

制定价格

任何商品的定价都基于以下两点：即生产商品的成本，以及人们愿意为这个商品所支付的价格。有些产品被认为是"价格敏感型的"，关于这类商品，有些是生活必需品，如牙膏，人们每天都要用到，但是认为它价值并不高；另一些则是奢侈品，它们的价格往往与价值无关。

供给与需求

供求关系指的是一种市场运作的方式——人们如何决定他们愿意购买的某种商品的数量。

如果供给和需求是平衡的，那么愿意购买某一种商品的人数将和愿意销售这一商品的人数相当。

需求或供给过大

但是，如果太多人想要购买商品，而商品的供应有限，或者很难买到这种商品，那么问题就来了：由于商品的稀缺，这类商品的价格就会上涨，但是价格上涨会导致购买者的成本太高，这样，购买者的需求就会下降；而需求下降又会导致卖家生意惨淡，甚至有可能破产。

合适的价格

因此,制定出一个合适的价格是非常重要的,以确保人们愿意以这个价格来购买商品。任何商品的价值都是人们愿意为它支付的价值。但是,大部分商品也都有一个市场价值——它是建立在人们通常准备为类似商品支付的价格的基础之上的。

价格始终是重要的。人们用于消费的钱是有限的,如果他们在某一种商品上花费了过多的钱,那么,他们在另一种商品上就不能再花钱了。如果某一种商品的价格上涨了,那么,其他竞争性的商品或者更便宜的商品就会卖得更好。

讨价还价

讨价还价是让商品价格降低的一种办法。从某种意义上说,讨价还价这件事,每个人都会做。当然,国际贸易商所做的通常并不叫"讨价还价",他们所做的事被叫做"谈判"。每个人都希望能够支付最优惠的价格,所以,这往往意味着你给出的价格是卖方愿意考虑的价格。

卖家可能会想要商品价格再高一点,于是买家就会提高一点点,慢慢地,通过这种讨价还价的方式,最终买卖双方就会选取一个折中的价格,这样双方都会满意。

黄 金

黄金是一种贵重金属，它的价值在于它的柔软性，以及它的韧性。这也意味着它可以不打碎就能够很容易地被制成许多细小的金属丝。它也非常重，它的重量是同等体积的水的19倍；而且与大多数金属不同，大多数金属被加热后都会软化，但是黄金却不会轻易地吸收热量，因此，即使在非常热的状态下，它也仍然能够保持原状。

克拉黄金

黄金是用"克拉"这个单位来衡量的。这个名字来自于一种古老的度量方法，比如说1克拉，它相当于一颗角豆的重量。

克拉现在用于判断黄金的纯度。24克拉黄金是纯度最高的一种黄金。

黄金是一种贵重金属

金本位制

千百年来，黄金一直是价值的标准，是货币尺度的基础。黄金有助于各国之间进行贸易。如果一个国家实行的是金本位制，那么，它可以按需要把本国的货币兑换成黄金，并且同意以固定价格买入或卖出黄金。到1900年，所有的主要国家在相互进行贸易的时候，都采用了金本位制。

黄金储备

如今，货币是建立在美元价值的基础之上的，而不是基于全世界的宝贵的黄金储备。但是，黄金仍然是一种非常有价值的金属。之前，当黄金还是一种最重要的货币衡量尺度时，各国政府都大量囤积黄金，但如今，它们都躺在了金库里。

1980年的时候，世界黄金的价格达到了顶峰，但是在今天，黄金的价格只值1980年的1/4了。由于黄金价格的下跌，各国政府都在重新考虑它们的黄金库存量。英国、瑞士、荷兰、比利时、加拿大、阿根廷和澳大利亚等国的中央银行，全都已经售出了大量的库存黄金，甚至像澳大利亚和加拿大这样的主要黄金生产国，也在销售黄金。

谁在储存黄金？该储存多少？

美国的金库里有世界上最多的黄金储备——大约储存着7 500 000公斤的黄金。

其中，最大的一块金条重达200公斤，它是由日本的三菱综合材料株式会社于1999年12月铸造的。这块黄金的纯度为99.99％，宽19.5厘米，底长40.5厘米，高16厘米。

三菱综合材料株式会社铸造的金条

银行业务

一直以来,世界各国银行对全世界贸易和工业的发展起到了重要的推动作用,它们使得商人、制造商以及其他厂商之间的资金往来变得更为便捷;如果没有世界各国银行的贡献,我们这个世界有可能完全不一样。

银行的起源

对早期的商人来说,不幸的是,这个世界并不如现在这般安全。如果他们随身携带大量的金钱,那么,他们就有可能会让自己陷入危险的境地,比如有可能遭遇抢劫。

但是后来,在意大利北部,一些贵族家庭在各个不同的城市设立了银行代理商。它们允许客商把钱存入自己家乡所在的城市的银行里,以换取一张"信用证"。这张信用证能够随身携带,并且在任何一个城市的银行里都能兑换成真正的钱。

有了银行之后,商人们面临的另外一个问题就不是问题了,即当他们需要筹集一大笔资金,以用来雇用船只、购买货物时,他们可以不必使用自己的钱,而是向银行借款。当然,这需要支付部分利息给银行。

银行投资者

今天,许多大银行在世界各国和地区都设有分支机构,它们进行大笔金额的交易,并投资于外币、小企业和大公司。

中国上海的金融中心,它拥有多家令人印象深刻的高耸入云的银行和金融大厦

庞大的银行业

现在世界各国的每一个大城市都会有一个金融中心,许多公司都在那儿开展金融业务。但有一些国家的城市金融中心会比其他国家的城市金融中心更大,也更有影响力。现在银行业已经是每个国家商业生活的重要组成部分了,银行家们所做出的决策,使得每一秒钟都会有巨额资金在全球流动。

世界银行

世界银行并不是一个真正意义上的银行,它是联合国的一个机构,获得了184个不同国家的支持。这些国家共同努力,以确保世界银行有足够的资金,同时也控制着世界银行花钱的方式。这些国家齐心协力成立世界银行的目的,是为了能够及时地帮助那些世界上较为贫穷的国家。

摆脱贫困

世界银行声明:"我们的梦想是一个没有贫穷的世界。"这也是它的使命。我们生活在这样一个世界里:有些国家连普通人都非常富裕,这些国家的人均年收入超过了4万美元;而与此同时,在一些最为贫困的国家里,一个普通人的收入每年只有700美元。这两个数字的差距实在是太大了!在我们这个星球上,最贫穷的人不仅遭受粮食短缺之苦,而且还缺失教育、医疗卫生、水和电,而这些是最基本的生活必需品。

救援

为此,世界银行伸出了援助之手,它发放贷款,提供补助金,并为穷人们提供技能培训。世界上最富有的40个国家,每年都会拿出数十亿美元,去帮助那些世界上最贫穷的26个国家的人们,以改善他们的生活,让他们的生活变得更美好。

近些年来,世界银行同时在实施的援助项目都超过2 000个。除此之外,总还是不断会有新的紧急情况出现需要它去资助。它赞助了很多项目,比如给贫穷国家和地区的人民打急需用的水井和装置供水系统等。

新的水井为村民们带来了干净的水

孤儿们在学校里吃饭并接受教育

新的学校将为大家带来教育机会

货物正从慈善组织的仓库里派发出去

IMF（国际货币基金组织）

IMF是国际货币基金组织的代称，虽然它也不是严格意义上的银行，但它是一个筹集和分配巨额资金的机构。它拥有1 210亿美元的资金。这是一个多么庞大的数字啊！

但是，它把钱借给谁呢？为什么要出借呢？跟世界银行一样，国际货币基金组织致力于帮助世界各地的国家，它的工作对象涵盖了所有的国家，无论贫富。它希望为了全球的利益，大家都能够一起工作和贸易。如果各国相互合作，发展贸易，那么，我们这个世界将更加充满信心，也更加稳定。

国际货币基金组织（IMF）的目的：
* 促进国际货币和汇率的稳定。
* 帮助扩大国际贸易的均衡增长。
* 帮助建立各个国家间更便捷的支付系统。

使用同一种货币

在欧洲，有一些国家相互合作、彼此贸易，甚至共用同一种货币，它们就是欧洲联盟当中的19个国家。这些国家称它们自己为欧元区。

ECB

ECB 指的是欧洲中央银行。众所周知，欧洲中央银行是欧洲单一货币欧元的中央银行。

欧元是一种新的货币。它是1999年开始在12个欧洲国家率先使用的，这些国家不再分别使用法郎、里拉和马克以及其他货币。现在其他一些国家也加入进来了。

欧洲央行的主要任务是确保欧元的稳定，这就意味着它要时刻关注各个同盟国的商品价格，以确保1欧元的货币不管在哪儿使用都能买到相同数量的商品。因此，如果一杯咖啡在法国价格为1欧元，那么，它在欧元区的任何地方都应该是1欧元。

共用欧元的国家

以下19个国家共用欧元

* 奥地利
* 比利时
* 塞浦路斯
* 爱沙尼亚
* 芬兰
* 法国
* 德国
* 希腊
* 爱尔兰
* 意大利
* 拉脱维亚
* 卢森堡
* 马耳他
* 荷兰
* 葡萄牙
* 斯洛文尼亚
* 斯洛伐克
* 西班牙
* 立陶宛

单一货币

与其他国家共用同一种货币意味着什么呢？这些国家的人们语言各异，彼此远隔千里，他们都有各自不同的生活，同样也做着不同的工作。

事实证明，单一货币体系远比许多人在1999年时所想象得更为困难，施行起来也更容易失败。

正在建设中的智能化的、新的欧洲央行总部

共用同一种货币真的好吗？

好的地方：

✻ 贸易变得更加便利了，因为再也不需要兑换货币了。

✻ 某个国家货币贬值的风险也不复存在了。

✻ 欧洲的公民能够到欧洲的任何一个国家去搜寻某一种商品的最优惠的价格。

✻ 劳动力和货物可以在欧洲各国之间进行更为自由的流动。

✻ 货币由欧洲央行管理，它不受任何一个特定国家的影响。

不好的地方：

✻ 这个系统对较大的欧元区国家更为有利，而对较小的欧元区国家则不是太为有利。

✻ 如果欧元区的某些国家陷入太多的债务当中，那么，它们有可能会给本区内的其他国家带来一些负面影响。

✻ 欧元走强会提高欧元区商品的购买价格，这样不利于出口。

世界财富

世界上有富有的人，也有富有的国家。他们因为与其他国家进行贸易而变得富有，他们有可能卖的是原材料，比如说铁矿和木材，或者有可能卖的是他们国家一些人的某些特殊的技能。

国内生产总值（GDP）

一个国家的富裕程度，是通过生活在这个国家的人在任何一年内，对国家的总体财富的贡献多少来衡量的，或者是通过他们赚了多少钱来衡量的。这个衡量标准就叫作国内生产总值，简称GDP。

美国是一个绝佳的例子。它拥有大量的自然资源，并且利用这些自然资源使国家变得富有了。中东的一些小国家因为出口宝贵的石油资源而变得很富有。卢森堡是一个小小的非工业化国家，但是那里住着许多富有的人。这主要是因为它的税收政策。

最富有的国家和地区

* 卡塔尔
* 卢森堡
* 新加坡
* 挪威
* 文莱达鲁萨兰国
* 中国香港
* 美国
* 阿拉伯联合酋长国
* 瑞士
* 澳大利亚
* 加拿大
* 奥地利
* 爱尔兰
* 荷兰
* 瑞典
* 冰岛
* 中国台湾
* 德国
* 科威特
* 丹麦

美国、阿根廷和澳大利亚有大量的草原可供饲养牛,它们的牛肉出口到世界各国

生活成本

有些国家可能很富有,但是它们的生活成本也很高。它们被称为高生活成本的国家。

如果你想赚钱,但又想低成本地生活,那么就避免去以下这些国家和地区:

* 日本
* 韩国
* 俄罗斯
* 中国台湾
* 挪威
* 中国香港
* 瑞士
* 丹麦
* 阿根廷
* 中国

韩国拥有巨大的船舶工业。它的船只销往全球各地

卡塔尔、文莱、阿拉伯联合酋长国、科威特拥有丰富的石油资源,它们把石油销售到世界各国

七国集团（G7）

"七国集团（G7）"是一个术语，它特指世界上工业和商业最发达的七个国家。

携手合作，共同发挥作用

七国集团的目的是，通过召开年度首脑会议，以及各种政策会议和研讨会，来讨论世界的经济和政治形势。这些会议和研讨会的结果也会对世界经济和政治形势产生影响。会议的地点通常设在各成员国，但每年都会改变。

最近，一年一度的七国集团首脑会议主要关注并反对被认为是增长过快（过分追求高额利润）的大公司。有时候这些成员国看起来似乎对增加本国的财富更为感兴趣，甚至超过了帮助贫困国家提高社会财富的兴趣，然而，在一些大问题上，它们表现的意见却相当一致，比如说世界和平、携手合作以及化解各方矛盾冲突。

七国集团成员
* 加拿大
* 法国
* 德国
* 意大利
* 日本
* 英国
* 美国

正在崛起的大国

或许七国集团的成员国已经开始变得落后了，新兴的富裕国家正在崛起。中国对世界经济增长的贡献是欧元区12国的3倍，印度也不甘落后。目前，世界经济正在发生着翻天覆地的变化，各经济大国都参加到了世界经济事务中，因此，现在出现了一个更大的全球性组织，它由19个国家再加上欧盟组成。

这个组织的成员国有
* 澳大利亚
* 印度
* 阿根廷
* 法国
* 中国
* 加拿大
* 俄罗斯
* 巴西
* 德国
* 印度尼西亚
* 沙特阿拉伯
* 南非
* 墨西哥
* 意大利
* 日本
* 美国
* 土耳其
* 英国
* 韩国
* 欧盟

加速发展

事物随时都在不断地发生变化。当较为富裕的国家出现问题时，它们的经济增长就有可能减缓、停滞甚至更糟（请参见下图中淡蓝色和淡黄色的部分）。而较贫穷的国家大多在非洲、南美洲和亚洲，由于受益于国外的援助和投资，这些国家的经济已经开始增长了，而且增长得很快（请参见下图中橙色和红色的部分）。

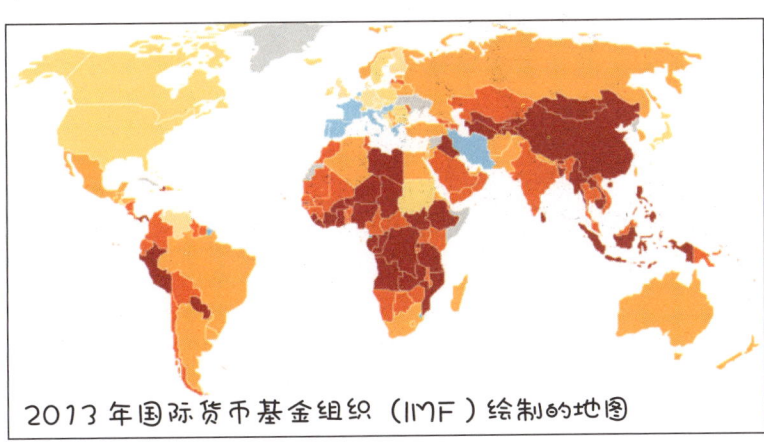

2013年国际货币基金组织（IMF）绘制的地图

世界贫困

就像人一样,某个特定的国家也可以被认为是贫穷的。一个贫穷的国家可能是人均GDP很低的国家,也可能是自然资源相当贫乏的国家,还有可能是没有能力出口货物来赚钱的国家。贫穷背后的原因之一可能是自然因素造成的,比如天气、土壤成分、地形和地貌等。如果一个国家的绝大多数土地是沙漠,那么便很难种植出足够的东西来养活全国人民,更不用说有多余的物品供出口了。贫穷背后的原因之二,也可能是这个国家没有任何矿产资源(比如金属)和石油可供开采和出售。

数以百万计的人生活于贫困当中

贫穷的意思并不是说,你无法为你所处的社会做出贡献。贫穷仅意味着:资源匮乏、教育缺失以及你健康不佳;你生活在恶劣的环境当中,比如你的周围是繁忙而拥挤的道路、工厂,甚至是废品堆放场;你甚至有可能需要到垃圾场中去寻找食物,或者通过捡垃圾而谋生。

贫穷意味着你没有尊严地生活着,对未来的希望十分渺茫。全世界大约有10亿人生活在令人绝望的条件之下。

世界上最贫穷的国家和地区

* 海地
* 尼泊尔
* 南苏丹
* 科摩罗
* 几内亚比绍
* 莫桑比克
* 埃塞俄比亚
* 几内亚
* 多哥
* 马里
* 阿富汗
* 马达加斯加
* 马拉维
* 尼日尔
* 中非共和国
* 厄立特里亚
* 利比里亚
* 布隆迪
* 津巴布韦
* 刚果（金）

它们为什么会这么贫穷呢？

有些国家之所以贫穷，原因有很多，其中气候是一个重要原因。在许多情况下，贫穷是由于恶劣的气候条件和突发性的自然灾害共同作用的结果。还有些国家的城市人口过多，也是一个原因。生活在城市中的许多人无法找到工作，甚至没有一个栖身之地。

用废弃物拼凑而成的破破烂烂的家

像这样的贫民窟是人体各种疾病的温床

没有资源

一个贫穷的国家之所以贫穷，或许还因为可用的资源太少，它既不能在本国资源的基础上发展本国经济，也无法把资源出口到国外去，更没有机会与国际市场接轨。在许多贫穷国家，根本不存在现代工业。然而，世界上很多的富裕国家就是通过工业化而创造财富的。此外，有些贫穷的国家一直依赖于一些价值不断在下降的商品，这也是贫穷的一个原因。

在我们这个星球上，还有12亿人的生活费每天不足1美元。

让世界更平等

债务对这些贫穷的国家不会有任何帮助。多年以来,许多贫穷的国家都在向富裕的国家借钱,它们借钱的目的是为了养活自己国家的人民,有时候甚至是为了支付战争费用。

第三世界国家债务

我们都知道当我们欠债无法偿还时意味着什么,即使我们欠债的对象是我们自己的母亲。但是,如果借钱者是一个国家,那么,当它还不起拖欠其他国家的债务时,又会怎么样呢?

在2000年年初,世界银行列出了42个负债的国家。这些国家有时候被称为重债穷国。许多重债穷国的负债数额实在是太大了,以至于连债务利息都无法全部偿还,更不用说是债务本金了。

更加糟糕的是,这些国家把那些原本应该用于卫生健康事业、教育事业以及建设事业的钱,全都拿来还债了。

免除债务

有些事情已经迫在眉睫而不得不做了,于是,在1996年,一些债权国最终一致同意,贫穷国家需要摆脱它们的债务负担,而要做到这样,债权国只需简单地抹去债务记录或者"忘记"债务就可以了。

免除债务计划的成功

为了获得免除债务的资格,这些重债穷国必须把它们原本用于偿还债务的钱,拿来用在摆脱饥饿和贫困上。

今天,在列名单中的40个重债穷国,其中有32个国家已经被世界银行和国际货币基金组织成功地免除了债务。

援助

有些国家甚至已经取得了更大的成功。排名前10位的经济增长最快的国家包括安哥拉、缅甸、埃塞俄比亚、柬埔寨、尼日利亚和卢旺达,所有这些国家都是当前最大的受援国。世界银行的博客指出,当今大多数的低收入国家将在2025年达到人均中等收入水平。

少量的现金能够帮助农民们种植庄稼并且获得丰收,进而把多余的农产品用于出售

给予知识

也许再也没有国家、机构或组织贷款给贫穷国家了。现在大家一致认为,帮助重债穷国的人民让他们接受教育、进行技能培训和提高知识水平,远比给它们现金管用得多。

公平贸易

多年以来，富裕国家生产的粮食已经远远超过了它们自己的所需。但是，这些富裕国家并不是告诉它们的农民少生产粮食，而是坚持认为应该把这些多余的大量的糖、小麦和水稻卖给这些贫穷国家——以特别便宜的价格。

"施舍物"

听起来，这种做法像是给贫穷国家的一种施舍，似乎会对它们有所帮助，但事实上毫无助益。进口食品的价格比贫穷国当地生产的产品的价格要便宜，因此，虽然富裕国家的农民处理掉了他们多余的库存商品，并且从中获得了收益，但贫穷国家的农民却因此而失去了生意并蒙受损失。

公平贸易组织的标志

这并不公平

大型企业可能不会受此影响，因为它们的财富让它们拥有了巨大的权力，大到足以影响政府决策的地步。当然，这是不公平的！

因此，一些规模较小的公司建立了一个被称为公平贸易的体系。在公平贸易中，农民和其他供应商能够为他们所提供的商品争取到一个公平的支付价格。

公平和绿色

你会仔细考虑你所购买的东西吗？你是一个"绿色购物者"吗？

就像公平贸易一样，绿色购买把我们带回到了道德层面上。它倡议我们购买健康的商品，或者让我们不要去购买会导致南美洲的热带雨林受到破坏的商品。如果我们每个人都能够一起努力，那么，大家的力量就足以对我们赖以生存的环境带来巨大的益处。我们购买的所有东西归根结底都是来自地球的，而且我们一直都在以这样或那样的方式影响着地球，尽管我们并不一定能够直接看到结果。

香蕉种植户携手合作，与全球的采购商签订了公平贸易协定

绿色购买

绿色购买并没有那么容易做到，这不仅因为你可能要为此多付出一些钱，而且还因为绿色产品的销售点很难找到。但是，如果你想购买那些对地球有益的商品，那么，你就可以加入数以百万计的想改变现状的人群当中。

谨慎购买

贸易咖啡公司是一家能够确保种植咖啡的农民的收入不会过低的公司。你可以在许多商店和咖啡馆买到这家公司的咖啡。

美体小铺是另外一家公司，当它向供货商购买化妆品原材料时，会确保供货商获得一个合理的报酬。

灾 难

大体上，任何一个国家都可能会时不时地遭受某些灾难的侵袭。这些灾难有可能是洪水、地震，甚至还有可能是战争。各种各样的灾难都会迅速地对一个国家的商业和贸易产生影响，甚至还有可能影响到国家机构正常运行的能力。

干旱……

不幸的是，对于自然灾害，除非在它发生之后，否则，在面对时，人们一般都是无能为力的。北部和中部非洲的许多地方都有干旱的历史，现在和过去唯一的区别是，现在干旱是每5年发生一次，而不是每10~15年发生一次，而且比以往更为严重。干旱带来的是粮食的歉收和饥荒。

……饥荒

还有一些原因也会导致饥荒，比如说，快速的人口增长，较小的农场规模，落后的耕作方式，人们过度砍伐森林，贫瘠的土壤，等等。

例如，现在的埃及南部国家，每年都有20亿吨的表层土要么被吹走，要么沿着蓝色尼罗河被冲到埃及。这些表层土都来自埃及南部国家的可耕作土地，农民们要依靠它们来种植庄稼，而现在它们却被带到了这里。

食物援助

考虑到人口规模，我们很容易就可以搞清楚，为什么像干旱这样的自然灾害会导致如此严重的后果，许多国家仍然需要依靠食物援助来养活自己千千万万的人民。

战争

一旦爆发战争——无论这种战争是国与国之间还是国家内部各组织之间——战争各方都会在士兵和军事装备上花费数百万美元，而这些美元原本都是可以用来购买食物的。据估计，全世界各地的战争导致每天都要花去数百万美元。

战争除了给人们的生活带来痛苦、恐惧和动荡不安之外，它还占用了许多人力资源。而这些人力资源本来是可以用来发展国家经济和提高人们生活水平的。

一个人被派去打仗，他就不能为国家的经济增长和繁荣贡献自己的力量了

战争难民被迫住进了临时营地

战争中

目前还处于战争中的国家包括
* 南苏丹
* 黎巴嫩
* 伊拉克
* 叙利亚
* 肯尼亚
* 也门民主共和国
* 刚果
* 菲律宾
* 印度
* 阿富汗
* 哥伦比亚
* 马里
* 埃及
* 索马里
* 尼日利亚
* 利比亚
* 土耳其
* 俄罗斯
* 乌克兰
* 以色列
* 斯里兰卡
* 乌干达
* 缅甸

相互帮助

也许你的生活非常舒适和安逸,之前你对外面的世界一无所知。但是现在每天电视和报纸的新闻都会报道说,外面的世界存在着许多问题和不公正之处。如果你关心世界的发展,关心地球上的其他人,想成为一个"地球公民",那么现在就应该放眼世界了。

慈善组织

慈善组织是这样一些组织,即它们总是以各种不同的方式去帮助那些需要帮助的人。你或许知道许多大型的慈善组织,或许你还时不时地受到过它们的帮助呢!这些组织的成员会在第一时间里奔赴灾区,并给予当地紧急救助。这些组织大多获得了极好的口碑。无论它们被设在何地,它们都长期致力于促进改善教育和医疗卫生事业。

孩子们在学校里学习技能

UNICEF

UNICEF是指联合国儿童基金会,它是一个为儿童争取权利的慈善机构。它不分性别,为所有儿童提供良好的基础教育。有些国家在教育方面并没有给予女孩同等的待遇。健康项目也很重要。联合国儿童基金会致力于让尽可能多的儿童都有机会注射拯救生命的疫苗。被剥削或被虐待的儿童是这个组织优先救助的对象,一些国家的儿童被迫入伍或成为童工,他们的工作时间很长,但是报酬却很低。

红十字会

红十字会和红新月会是世界上最大且独立的人道主义国际联合会运动组织机构，它拥有一亿多成员。这个组织努力做到对世界各地的灾难和冲突迅速地做出反应。它为受灾的民众提供食物、水、住所和医疗用品，它也培训医生、护士和修建医院，会针对许多人道主义问题（例如禁止布设地雷）提出自己的建议。

救助儿童会

救助儿童会在全世界40个国家都有它的足迹。它的目的是帮助一些贫穷的家庭改善儿童健康状况并给他们提供接受教育的机会，它同时也提供必要的现金资助。它能够迅速地救助那些陷于灾难之中的儿童，比如在海啸、地震和战争中受灾的儿童。

在有些地方，比如说在苏丹，慈善组织会给当地居民分发一些基本的食物，如大米、牛奶和面包等。在那里，由于干旱的气候条件，造成了当地居民营养不良，同时还给他们带来了其他疾病。

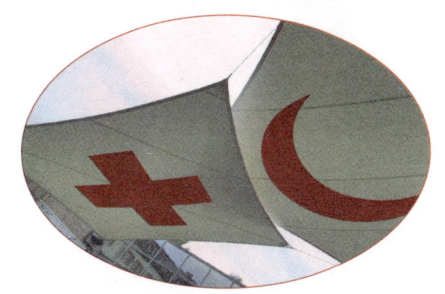

红十字和红新月会的标志

红十字会志愿者正在准备救援用的食物

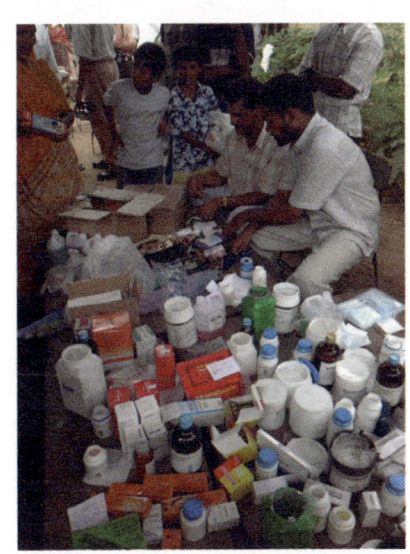

医疗用品总是需要的

快乐的财富

世界银行在全球拥有180个成员国，它通常是根据这些成员国所拥有的货币财富来判断它们的富裕程度的。但是，现在它还要衡量其他一些东西，比如教育经费、人权记录和人均预期寿命，同时还要衡量一国的文化价值、民众的自我价值实现程度和群体参与情况。

国民幸福总值并不等于国内生产总值

不丹是喜马拉雅山脚下的一个海拔较高的多山王国。这个国家的民众甚至走得更远。他们如今的统治者是吉格梅·辛格·旺楚克国王，他认为，幸福感远比财富更重要。不丹是世界上唯一一个用国民幸福总值（GNH）来衡量福祉的国家。

优先考虑的事情

大多数国家的政府首脑都对自己国家买卖东西的能力心存忧虑，担心自己的国力是否能够负担得起它所需要的东西。但是不丹并非如此。它的国王旺楚克认为，如果他的国家试图发展经济，与其他国家接轨，那么就会牺牲掉他们古老的传统、遗产和文化，以及美丽的山区环境。在不丹，民众优先考虑的确实是幸福感，而不是经济财富。

简单生活价值观

某些宗教的教规认为,幸福并不是由人们所拥有或占有的东西来决定的。虽然这可能有助于减轻人们因贫困带来的痛苦和鼓励人们慷慨大方,但是摆脱贫困还得靠我们的知识、想象力和生活技能。

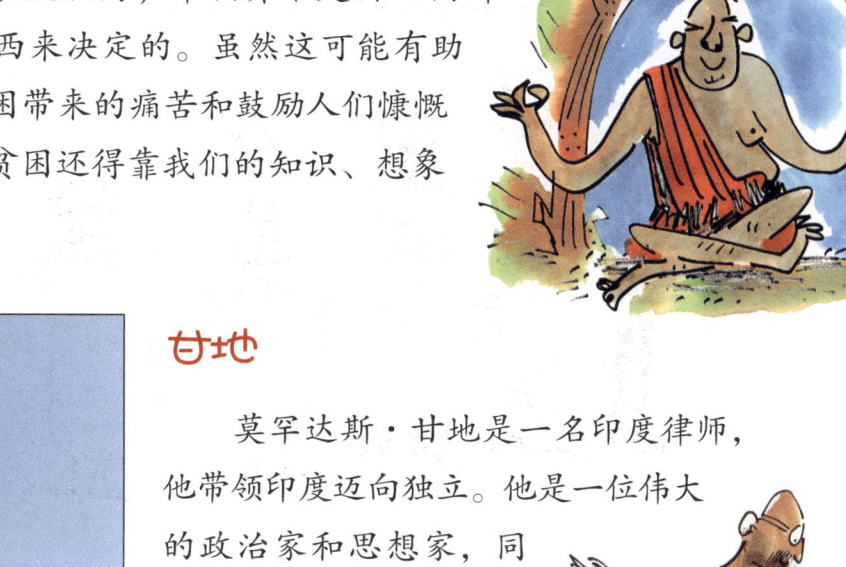

甘地

莫罕达斯·甘地的雕像

莫罕达斯·甘地是一名印度律师,他带领印度迈向独立。他是一位伟大的政治家和思想家,同时也是简单生活价值观的一个象征。他认为,过简单生活会比追求金融财富更能给人带来快乐。

那么,到底谁是正确的呢?

能用生产能力和消费能力来判断一个国家的富裕程度吗?或者能以生活于这个国家的人的生活质量和幸福感来判断吗?我们应该更看重某些东西吗,比如说干净的水、绿色的森林、洁净的空气、传统的生活方式?如果一个国家通过砍伐森林来获取财富,那么,这难道不应该把砍伐森林造成的损失从它的财富中扣除吗?

联合的世界

携手合作

我们都希望看到一个和平稳定的世界，并且在这个世界上，每个人无论出身和背景怎样，都有机会过上自己最想要的生活。但是不幸的是，贫穷无处不在，数亿人生活在贫穷之中，甚至在世界上最富裕的国家中也有穷困潦倒的人。

在这个世界上，有这么多的财富、这么多的钱，怎么还会有那么多贫穷的人存在呢？这真是一件令人难以置信的事情。像国际货币基金组织这样的机构，正在尽它自己最大的努力去创造一个更加平等的世界，但是这并不容易！

你能帮忙吗？

你可能会认为，世界如此之大，自己又是如此渺小，对于世界上的大部分事情我们自己都是无能为力的，所以我们很容易就会耸耸肩说，我们真的没办法。但是，我们要知道，世界上的许多事情都有一个开端——一个重要的开端。

现在你知道了……

……去做慈善事业，特别是当灾难发生时，哪怕是你小小的一点捐助，都有可能改变一个人的命运。如果你拒绝购买由童工生产的产品，那么，你就是在帮助制止这种使用童工的做法。如果你寻找并购买有公平贸易标志的食品，那么，你就是在帮助那些有需要的贸易商。

金钱不是万能的

你现在已经知道了，虽然钱能够让我们的世界充满活力，但是其他一些东西也可能并且确实也能够做到这一点，它们与金钱同样重要。

中英文术语对照表

3rd world debt 第三世界债务
世界上较贫穷的国家欠世界上较富裕的国家的钱。

aid 援助
通常是指被送往需要帮助的比较贫穷的国家的金钱、食品、药品和其他物品。

balance of payments 国际收支平衡表，国际收支差额
一个国家出口额与进口额之间的差额。

Brand 品牌
制造商产品的标志或名称，很容易被识别出来。

charity 慈善组织，慈善机构
为有需要的人提供金钱或帮助的组织。

commodity 商品
主要指一些比较重要的产品，如谷物和金属等世界上进行大量买卖的产品。

currency 货币
某一特定国家所使用的钱。

debt 债务
借来需要偿还的钱。

economy 经济
贸易和工业体系的总称，通过它来创造和使用国家财富。

export 出口
生产国把商品出售给其他国家。

Fair Trade 公平贸易
是一个由买方和卖方所组成的体系，同意以公平、公正的价格成交商品。在商店出售的公平贸易商品都有标记。

GDP
国内生产总值的简称。

government 政府
由民众选举而产生的、代表民众管理国家的一群人所组成的机构。

import 进口
从海外购进商品。

Legal tender 法定货币
指一个国家所使用的货币，它包括硬币和纸币，是这个国家法律所承认的用于交易的货币。

market value 市场价值
在某一特定时间出售的商品的价格。

merchant 商人
以盈利为目的的大批量买卖商品的人或企业，他们通常与其他国家开展对外交易。

natural resource 自然资源
存在于自然界中的、能够被人们利用的、用于制造其他产品的原料，如水、煤和木材等。

povery 贫穷
指人们没有足够的钱、无法满足基本需求的一种状态。

price 价格
人们购买物品的成本，通常它能够反映出人们购买的物品的生产成本，以及人们为购买它时所支付的体现价格的货币金额。

specialisation 专业化
指在一个特殊的生产领域，某个国家具有领先的专业水平，而且产品可以用来出口。

supply and demand 供给与需求
是一种状态，它指商品的价格取决于人们能够获得多少这种东西以及有多少人愿意购买这种东西。

tariff 关税
是进口国针对进口的货物和服务征收的一种税，目的是以此来提高进口商品的价格，从而起到限制贸易的作用。

trade gap 贸易赤字
是指一个国家的进口额大于出口额时的状态。

索 引

3rd world debt 第三世界债务 48
ad valorem tax 从价税 31
aid 援助 45，49，52
amber 琥珀 12
balance of payments 国际收支平衡，国际收支平衡表 25
bank 银行 2，19，36，37，38，39，40，41，48，49，56
banknote 钞票 5，13，17
barter 易货 6，7
bead 珠子 12
Bhutan 不丹 14，56
bill of exchange 汇票 30
brand 品牌 28，60
carat 克拉 34
charity 慈善 39，54，55
child labour 童工 59
climate 气候 21，47
coin 硬币 5，12，13，17
Columbus 哥伦布 8
commodity 商品 21，47，60
container ship 集装箱船 11
cost 成本 19，22，31，32，60，61
cowrie shell 贝壳 12
currency 货币 2，13，14，16，17，18，19，37，41
customs 海关 30，31
debt 债务 41，48，49，60
denomination 面额 13
disaster 灾难 52，54，59

disease 疾病 55
dollar 美元 5，13，14，15，18，35，47
drought 干旱 52，55
duty 关税 22，30，31
eBay 易趣 23
economy 经济 3，24，45，47，53
education 教育 38，39，48，49，54，56
emergency 紧急情况 38
Euro 欧元 13，40
Europe 欧洲 12，13，40，41，45
European Union 欧盟 40
Eurozone 欧元区 40
export 出口 23
face value 面值，面额 13
fair trade 公平贸易 50，51，59
financial centre 金融中心 37
foreign currency 外汇 16
G7 七国集团 44，45
gold 黄金 12
gold reserve 黄金储备 35
gold standard 金本位，金本位制 34
government 政府 4，13，41，60，61
Gross Domestic Product (GDP) 国内生产总值（简称 GDP）42，46
Gross National Happiness 国民幸福总值，国民幸福指数 56
haggling 讨价还价 33
Heavily Indebted Poor Countries (HIPC) 重债穷国（简称 HIPC）48
heritage 遗产 56

import 进口 22，24，25
industry 工业，行业 36，43，47
International Monetary Fund (IMF) 国际货币基金（简称 IMF）39，45，49，58
internet 互联网 30
investment 投资 45，61
labour 劳动力 41
legal tender 法定货币 13
letter of credit 信用证 36
Magellan 麦哲伦 8
malnutrition 营养不良 55
Marco Polo 马可·波罗 8
market 市场 6，19，23，32，33
market value 市值 33
medium of exchange 交换媒介 7
merchant 商船 8
Mohandas Gandhi 莫罕达斯·甘地 57
natural disaster 自然灾害 47
natural resource 自然资源 46，47
negotiate 谈判 33
note 纸币 5，7，12，13，16，17
oil 石油 9，19，21，31，42，43，46
online trading 网上交易，在线交易 23
population 人口 46，52
port 港口 8，10，11
pound 英镑 14，15
poverty 贫穷 3，38，46，47，49，57，58，61
price 价格 2，30，32，33，34，35，40，41，60，61
product 产品 9，20，27，28，32，33，41，59，60，61
profit 利润 36，44，57

purchasing power 购买力 5
quota 配额 22
receipt 收据 12
Red Crescent 红新月会 55
Red Cross 红十字会 55
refugee 难民 53
Save the Children 救助儿童会 55
silver 银 12
specialisation 专业化 20
standard measure 衡量标准 12
supply and demand 供给与需求 32
surplus 盈余，剩余 6，49，50
tariff 关税 30，31
tax 税收 22，30，31，42，60，61
European Central Bank 欧洲中央银行 40
trade balance 贸易平衡 24
trade gap 贸易逆差 24
trade route 贸易路线
UNICEF 联合国儿童基金会 54
United Nations 联合国 38
unit of value 价值单位 7
Vasco da Gama 瓦斯科·达·伽马 8
war 战争 5，52，53
wealth 财富 3，4，23，42，44，47，50，56，57，58
World Bank 世界银行 38，39，48，49，56
world peace 世界和平 44
yuan 元 14，16，18
Zheng He 郑和 8

译后记

近年来，金融素养已成为培养孩子全面发展的一个重要方面。早在20世纪30年代，美国就开始了对中小学生进行与生活密切相关的理财教育。如今，美国中小学理财教育日趋成熟，主要围绕让中小学生正确地"认识钱、花钱、挣钱、借钱、分享钱以及让钱增值"而展开。在英国，随着金融理财教育的需求不断上升，金融监管局将个人理财知识纳入2008年实施的《国民教育教学大纲（修订）》中，要求中小学校必须对毕业生进行良好的金融知识教育。我国周边的国家如孟加拉、斯里兰卡等，也早已开设了此类课程。

中国的孩子也同样对生活中的金融知识充满渴求。2014年春节期间，《新京报》记者调查了北京90名10～13岁的孩子，结果发现，孩子们平均收到了4 867元压岁钱，比前一年上涨了5%，其中收得最多的孩子，压岁钱有2万元，而一半以上的孩子收到的压岁钱在1 000～5 000元之间。孩子们的压岁钱该怎么处理？一部分家长的做法是直接"据为己有"：要么存入自己的银行账户，要么用到家庭的日常开支及急需的事情上。虽然也有些家长孩子的主体意识和理财意识比较强，但多局限于将孩子的压岁钱存入银行、做定投基金和购买保险等方面。其实，多数孩子都渴望由自己来管理这笔数额不少的钱，但苦于没有一定的金融和理财知识，除了交给父母或买点零食、添加一些课辅用品等之外，也不知道怎么办。因此，及时地向他们普及金融知识，让他们学会理财，应该是时候了。

华夏出版社从英国引进的"华夏少儿金融智慧屋——货币系列"丛书（共4册，中英双语）确实是应时应景之作，它涉及四个主题——世界货币、国家货币、家庭理财和个人理财，它们相互补充，构成一个整体，以孩子们喜爱的绘本形式，把晦涩难懂的国际金融、货币、贸易、经济知识转化为生动有趣的语言，用最浅显的语言全面地阐述了"金融的逻辑"，让孩子们在轻松愉悦的阅读过程中全面触摸金融知识。

完成这一系列书，我要特别感谢我的儿子贾岚晴，这套书献给已是小学生的他。我还要感谢我的先生贾拥民，感谢他一直以来对我的支持、鼓励和帮助。感谢我的母亲蒋仁娟、父亲傅美峰对我儿子的悉心照顾，使我得以安心从事翻译工作。我的朋友和同事傅晓燕、鲍玮玮、傅锐飞、傅旭飞、陈贞芳、郑文英等，也给予了我很多支持和帮助，在此一并致以诚挚的谢意！

感谢华夏出版社一直以来对我的信任！

傅瑞蓉
2015年11月于杭州

附 英文影印版

小·贴士

小朋友,为了方便中英文对照阅读,我们排版时尽可能使中文和英文页码一一对应,但由于中英文表达习惯不同,有个别页码的尾行可能会出现不对应的情况,这时,你只要往后翻一页就会找到哦。——编者

Contents

4-5   **Who needs money?**
We all need money and the world wouldn't function without it.

6-7   **6,000 years of money**
Money in one form or another has been around a long time!

8-11   **Across the seas**
As trade spread between countries, money became international.

12-17   **World money**
Today, money looks different from country to country.

18-19   **Currency exchange**
What happens when we want to swap one country's money for another's?

20-31   **Trade**
Money swapping, or exchange, happens all the time as goods flow backwards and forwards overseas.

32-35   **Setting the price**
Can money be bought and sold like other goods?

36-41   **Bank to bank**
Banks across the world trade currencies and move money around.

42-45 World wealth
The wealthiest nations are those with successful economies – those who can manufacture and export and grow.

46-47 World poverty
Poorer nations often suffer from difficulties of all kinds. They need help to grow their trade and prosper.

48-55 Evening things out
How money can be moved around the planet by world organisations and small traders – to help nations, rich and poor, to trade and grow.

56-57 Happy wealth
Money doesn't always bring happiness. So how should a country value its economy?

58-59 United world
The world is not a peaceful place but there are many ways in which countries can reach out and help each other. We are all linked by trade and travel, and you are part of the 'link'.

60-61 Glossary
62-63 Index

Who needs money?

Everyone in the world uses money. It may look different in different countries, and it may have different names and entirely different values, but it will all work as money. And that's because each government decides what money can be legally used.

We all agree

Everyone who uses money – and as we know, that's everybody – accepts certain things about what money is:

* It's a unit for adding up the value of wealth.
* It's something you can exchange for stuff. You can buy and sell with it.
* It can be some kind of goods. You can buy and sell dollars or pounds just as you'd buy or sell coffee.
* You can reward people, give it away as a present, do what you like with it ...

... but everyone accepts that it has a **value**.

Day to Day

Everyone agrees about the value of their money when buying things. Generally, the value, or purchasing power, of each coin and each note doesn't change much from day to day. A dollar is a dollar and it buys more or less the same amount of something from one day to the next.

Of course, if something dramatic happens in a country, such as a war, the value of the coins and notes may suddenly change. Maybe food is short so you have to use more coins to buy a bag of rice than you did before. It doesn't always take a calamity for this to happen!

Trusting Money

So, we all have our own kind of money. And we trust it, and use it, and accept that it has a certain value. But do we trust and use each other's money? And why should we need to?

Well, there may be thousands of kilometres lying between us, but when it comes to trade, we generally need another country's money in order to pay for the stuff we buy in that country.

All money is really world money.

6,000 years of money

There's nothing new about world money. This is because there's nothing new about trade. Countries have been trading with each other for thousands of years, and that meant constantly swapping one kind of money for another as traders travelled about and bought and sold goods.

Barter

Swapping, or barter as it's known, is a good way for two people to get the things they want from each other. It's surprising that barter lasted so long and in so many societies.

From the point where early man settled in one place and grew crops, he often found he had too much of the things he'd grown, and too little of the things he hadn't. He needed to exchange his surplus goods for something he didn't have but needed. And this meant going to market and making a trade.

The earliest trade was just this – swapping one set of goods for another. Of course, both buyer and seller had to agree on a value for their goods – and both had to want what the other one had – which wasn't always easy.

Beyond the Village

At first, people bartered goods with the next village or tribe, but as they began to make more and more – of necessities such as pots and cloth, and luxuries such as jewellery and wine – traders travelled further and further to exchange goods. And as trade grew and barter became complicated, a better way was needed.

Coins take over

Eventually, money in the form of coins, and later notes, was introduced as the 'medium of exchange'. This meant that money became an accepted alternative to goods and had a value of its own. In other words, goods could now be 'swapped' or traded for money.

Pacify by Coin

Actually, coins were in use long before they replaced barter. Although they weren't used in trade, they were used to keep the enemy quiet. The verb 'to pay' comes from the Latin word "pacare" which originally meant to pacify, or make peace with. If a tribe wanted to make peace with another, it had to 'pay' for that peace by using a 'unit of value' acceptable to both sides.

And early coins were used to do this.

Across the seas

Just a few centuries on, trade was opening up the world. Now traders crossed oceans and continents, and established trade routes that crisscrossed the globe. Trade between countries began to expand.

The new merchants

Throughout the 1500s and 1600s, trade opened up both overland and across oceans, with great ports developing to become bustling merchant centres.

With foreign trade came a new group of merchants and adventurers. Merchants were exchanging goods for materials they didn't have locally. They sold goods to rich people, goods they had probably never seen before, and became rich themselves.

Back and Forth

In 1271, Marco Polo left Venice with his father and uncle to travel east towards China and the cities of the great Kublai Khan. They travelled the ancient 'silk road' to get there and stayed for 24 years. The Polos showed that trade between faraway countries was possible and profitable.

Later, European sea explorers like Columbus, Vasco da Gama and Magellan set sail towards the east, and then the west, to discover new lands and new trading possibilities.

Travelling in the opposite direction, the Chinese admiral, Zheng He, set off in ships with the most basic of charts and maps and nautical equipment. His was the largest fleet of ships ever recorded.

Exotic trade

They all hoped to discover new rich countries where they could gather up exotic local products – from tobacco, olive oil and spices, to gold and glassware, the scent frankincense, and exotic animals such as monkeys.

Goods for sale

foreign foods

oils and scents

exotic animals

gold and precious jewels

All these goods were new and exciting to the people back home.

Busy seas

It's easy to take for granted the silk clothes we buy that were made in China and Thailand, the tea we drink from India, the grapes flown in from Spain, or dad's car that was made in Japan. International trade is familiar to us all today.

Great trading ports

As trade grew, so did the world's great ports. Singapore became a link between east and west. European ports such as Genoa in Italy, Lisbon in Portugal, and London in England became stepping-off points for exploration as well as centres of trade and business.

Today, almost every country with a coastline or large river that enters the sea, has a large port.

Container ships

The goods are mostly brought across the seas on huge container ships. Containers can be piled high and make carrying goods much easier. A loaded container can simply be put onto a ship, truck or train without having to be emptied.

Great ports
Shanghai CHINA
Singapore SINGAPORE
Hong Kong CHINA
Busan SOUTH KOREA
Dubai UAE
Rotterdam NETHERLANDS
Kaohsiung TAIWAN CHINA
Hamburg GERMANY
Los Angeles USA

Money links us

Modern trade couldn't happen without money. So money holds us all together – working, spending, saving, travelling … In fact, money is the link between you and thousands of other people – absolute strangers – all of whom affect your life!

Let's find out how this can be.

World money

The fact is that money wasn't just invented in one place. It developed in all kinds of ways and in many different parts of the world. It started in one form and changed as country after country passed it around.

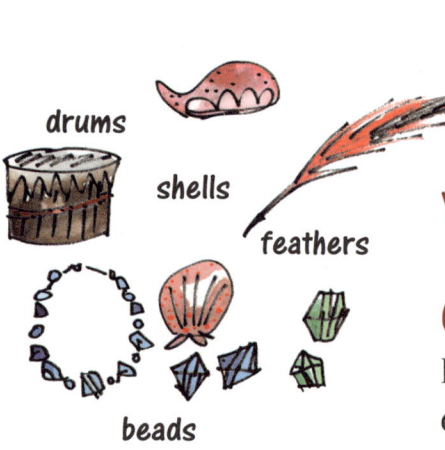

Early Roman coins showing Romulus and Remus, the twin founders of Rome.

Very early coins from Greece and Japan.

Bit and bobs

All sorts of crazy forms of money have cropped up in the past – amber, beads, cowrie shells, drums, eggs, feathers, to name but a few.

Valuable coins

It was only a matter of time before bits of silver and gold took over as a common exchange. Precious metals were chosen because they were valuable in their own right. They could act as a standard measure of value, so everyone would know how much an ox or duck was worth in gold coins.

Notes

Notes started out in Europe as receipts that people received when they deposited gold in the vaults of goldsmiths. The receipt was a promise to pay out the amount in gold when it was presented. These receipts soon became money in their own right and, eventually, the notes we use today.

Banknotes from top:
Nepal
Malaysia
Egypt
USA
Europe
China

MONEY WORDS

Currency
A generally accepted form of money, including notes and coins, issued by a government.

Denomination
Coins like the euro, Swiss franc and Australian dollar are some of hundreds of different world currencies. The value of the coin or note is printed clearly on it. This is known as its denomination.

Face value
This is an expression often used to emphasise that the value printed on the note or coin can be trusted.

Legal tender
This describes all the different denominations of a country's currency which have been adopted by that country's government for general use.

Your own money

Here are just some of the world's currencies with their special names.

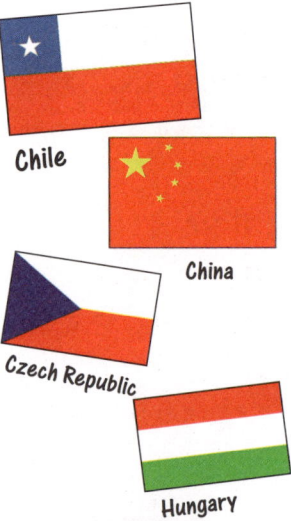

Afghanistan	**Afghan afghani**
Albania	**Albanian lek**
Algeria	**Algerian dinar**
Argentina	**Argentine peso**
Australia	**Australian dollar**
Azerbaijan	**Azerbaijani manat**
Bangladesh	**Bangladeshi taka**
Bhutan	**Bhutanese ngultrum**
Brazil	**Brazilian real**
Bulgaria	**Bulgarian lev**
Canada	**Canadian dollar**
Chile	**Chilean peso**
China, People's Republic of	**Chinese yuan renminbi**
Croatia	**Croatian kuna**
Czech Republic	**Czech koruna**
Denmark	**Danish krone**
Egypt	**Egyptian pound**
Hungary	**Hungarian forint**
Iceland	**Icelandic króna**
India	**Indian rupee**
Indonesia	**Indonesian rupiah**

14

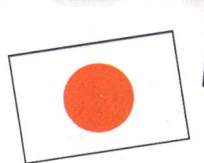
Japan

Iraq

South Africa

New Zealand

Pakistan

Peru

Philippines

Switzerland

Turkey

Ukraine

United Kingdom

Iran

South Korea

Malaysia

Morocco

Norway

Romania

Russia

Iran	Iranian **rial**
Iraq	Iraqi **dinar**
Japan	Japanese **yen**
Korea, South	South Korean **won**
Malaysia	Malaysian **ringgit**
Mexico	Mexican **peso**
Morocco	Moroccan **dirham**
New Zealand	New Zealand **dollar**
Norway	Norwegian **kroner**
Pakistan	Pakistani **rupee**
Peru	Peruvian **nuevo sol**
Philippines	Philippine **peso**
Romania	Romanian **leu**
Russia	Russian **rouble**
Saudi Arabia	Saudi **riyal**
South Africa	South African **rand**
Sweden	Swedish **krona**
Switzerland	Swiss **franc**
Thailand	Thai **baht**
Turkey	Turkish **lira**
Ukraine	Ukrainian **hryvnia**
United Kingdom	British **pound**
United States	United States **dollar**
Vietnam	Vietnamese **dong**

Saudi Arabia

Thailand

United States of America

Vietnam

Foreign exchange

It would be much easier if every country in the world had developed the same kind of coins and notes – we'd all be using a 'worldthalar' as the early science-fiction writers used to call it. But, as we know, every country has its own kind of money. And even when they call it by the same name, such as 'cent', it doesn't mean the actual value will be the same.

Buying currencies

If you're going on holiday to a foreign country, you'll need to buy foreign currency. For instance, if you're going to France you'll need euros, if you're going to the USA you'll need dollars, and if you're going to China you'll need yuan.

You can buy foreign currency at a bank – most banks have a foreign currency counter, or even at the post office, as long as the currency you want is not too unusual. The post office probably won't carry Albanian lek or Colombian pesos, but it will carry euros, dollars or pounds. Each seller will charge a fee for making the exchange, which might be a small percentage of the total with a minimum amount per transaction.

16

Foreign money

What happens when you come across a coin or bank note that's been issued in a different country? Is it still money? Yes, it certainly is, because it can buy things in the country in which it was issued. It can also be used to buy other currencies.

So, if you were given Japanese Yen, for example, you could use them to buy pounds or dollars or any other currency. This is called currency exchange.

Exchange boards show rates to buy and rates to sell for all the main currencies.

You can often change money at good rates in a local exchange shop.

Rate of exchange

You might get a better rate of exchange at a bank or online, than in a high street exchange shop. But be aware that exchange rates are different when you buy compared to when you sell. You'll always get a better rate when you buy. Money changers usually give both rates. So, it's best to get rid of all your foreign money before you return home.

17

Currency exchange

When countries want to trade with each other, they mostly want to buy and sell using their own currency. So, before international trading can take place, it has to be possible to trade currencies. For instance, if you wanted to buy lanterns from China, you'd have to pay in Chinese yuan. This means you'd have to be able to buy yuan with your pounds, dollars or pesos.

Use the Dollar

Nowadays, many countries set, or peg, the value of their money to the value of the American dollar, so this makes it easier. It's called a **fixed exchange rate**. This is how it works ...

Each country decides how much of their currency is worth 1 US dollar. It might look something like this: 1 Chinese yuan = 0.16 US dollar. This means you would need more than 6 Chinese yuan to buy a US dollar.

So, if a Chinese lantern costs 1 Chinese yuan, you will get 6 of them – and some change – when you offer the seller 1 dollar.

Sometimes, trade is made easier when traders agree to work in one currency, such as the dollar.

Floating Exchange Rate

Some currencies are said to 'float'. This means that the exchange rate value of a currency will change from day to day. The value of the currency depends upon **supply and demand** in the market. Some currencies are popular and people want to buy them or invest in them. Their value is high. Some are less popular and their value is low.

Buying and Selling Currencies

Each day, currency exchange rates are listed for everyone around the world to see. Banks and money changers, in fact everyone who works with money, all watch these lists carefully so they can swap currencies at the right rate.

Currencies are bought and sold just like goods such as wheat or oil. The money traders who do this work need to be alert, as the value of a currency can change from minute to minute.

If you buy 1,000 dollars in the morning, it may cost you more than if you buy them in the afternoon.

Trade

Most of what countries do with the money they earn involves buying and selling. Buying and selling is all about **trade** – using money to buy the things they need, and selling to people the things that they need. Trade is what keeps the money moving around.

A trade = an agreement

Because trade involves an exchange of goods that makes both the seller and the buyer happy, trade always involves an **agreement** or a **deal**. The final deal is absolute. You meet, you make a deal, you walk away. That's what trade is all about.

Specialisation

Thousands of years ago, when people first settled into villages and started farming, they got rid of their extra products by trading with other villages. At the same time, some villages became better at doing certain things than others – making arrowheads or woolly mammoth pendants. This is called **specialisation**, and it creates an even bigger demand for trade.

international trade

Today, the same thing applies on a far bigger scale. Countries, or nations, tend to concentrate on producing goods and services where they have a natural advantage over other countries.

Let's say there were only two countries: Saudi Arabia and Jamaica. Saudi Arabia produces more oil than it can possibly use. But it can't grow sugar cane and everyone wants sugar. Jamaica can grow loads of sugar cane because it has the right climate, but it needs oil for petrol, heating fuel and so on.

Providing there are no barriers to trading, Saudi Arabia can trade oil to Jamaica, while Jamaica can trade sugar to Saudi Arabia. They can exchange commodities, the products they have most access to.

An oil refinery lit up at night.

A sugar cane plantation in Jamaica.

This kind of specialisation in trade allows countries to sell goods and earn money to buy materials they may not be able to grow or find themselves.

it is called international trade.

Import – Export

Buying from each other

Goods and services that are brought into a country to sell are called imports. Imports cost nations money because the company that imports them has to pay for them. So, money moves out of the country.

Countries import goods or services, because they cannot produce them for themselves and they're necessary, or because they're cheaper to buy abroad than to manufacture at home.

Quotas

Most imports have some restrictions applied to them, such as an import tax, known as 'duty'. Often, only a certain amount of an item can be brought into a country. This is called a quota.

Let's say lots of workers in your country earn their living by making cars. If too many cheaper, foreign cars were allowed in, fewer local cars might be bought, and workers would lose their jobs. This kind of protection is sometimes necessary.

Selling to each other

Exports are goods and services that are supplied to and bought by companies or governments in other countries. Exporting, or selling lots of goods abroad, is good for a country because it brings cash in and creates wealth.

Money earned from exports benefits a country's wealth. Exports are usually paid for in the currency of the supplier. They may be goods and services that a country can produce easily or that are wanted by countries abroad.

America exports Nike shoes because they're popular, not because countries need them. However, America has large areas of land that are just right for wheat growing. So it exports wheat to countries that cannot grow wheat for themselves.

eBay

eBay is just one of many new ways that people across the world now trade with each other. They don't need to meet to do a deal – they do it online.

eBay is the largest online trading market in the world. Imagine over 100 million people all buying and selling to each other! It's just like a local street market – but in cyberspace. People not only buy and sell on this global auction site, but they chat and argue too, just like they did in the old marketplaces of hundreds of years ago.

As well as professional eBay sellers, millions of people add to their income by selling stuff on eBay.

Getting a balance

Sometimes you hear a newsreader telling you that the **trade balance** of your country is 'up or down'. The figures they give out are in millions of pounds, or even billions. You may wonder who's doing all this trading and why so much money is involved? Well, it's less complicated than you might think.

Keeping a balance

A country's trade balance is about what the country has sold abroad and what it has bought from abroad.

Most countries try to find a balance between their exports and their imports, so when they export a great deal, they also tend to import a great deal as well.

Together, all the money that flows in and out of a country is known as its **economy**.

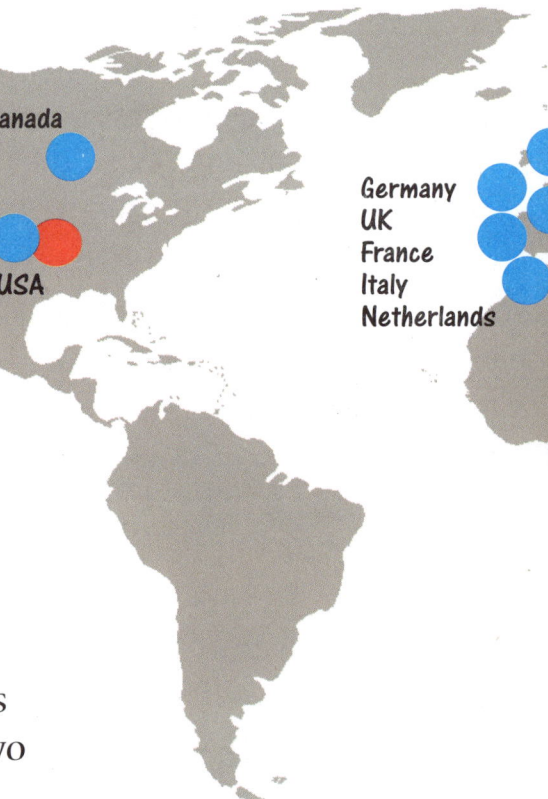

The trade gap

The difference between what a country sells and what it buys is the **trade gap**, and the two figures make up the **trade balance**.

24

The balance of payments

A **balance of payments** is a record used by governments to keep count of the money flowing into a country and the money flowing out. Keeping this type of record makes it possible for nations to determine if the current balance between imports and exports is acceptable, or if they need to take steps to change the balance. This record is kept year by year.

We are top importers
* United States
* Germany
* United Kingdom
* France
* Japan
* China
* Italy
* Canada
* Hong Kong China
* Netherlands

We are top exporters
* China
* United States
* Germany
* Japan
* France
* South Korea
* Netherlands
* Russia
* Italy
* United Kingdom

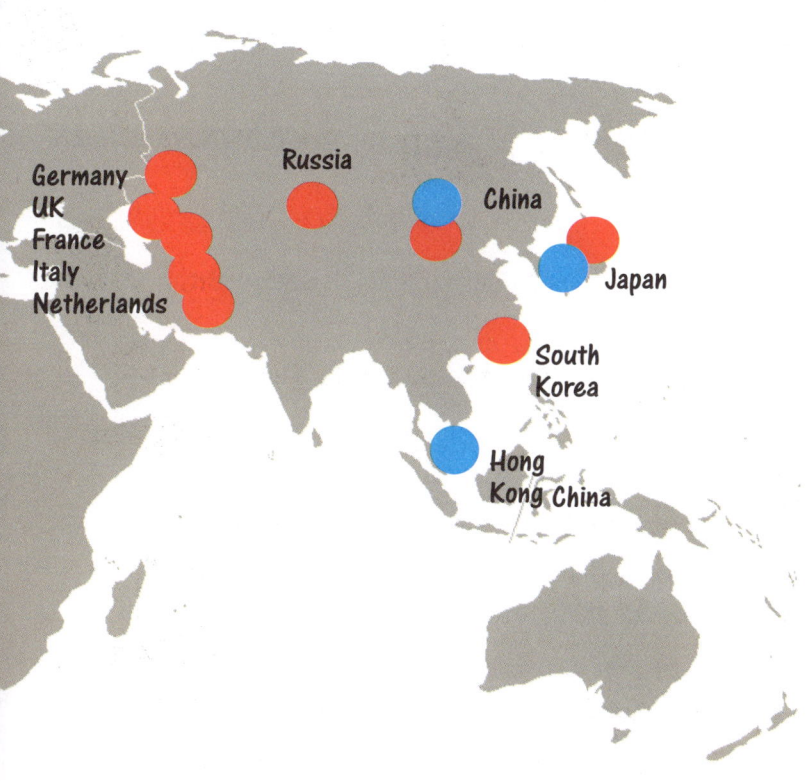

Who sells what?

These are the ten countries that sell the most goods around the world – and what they sell.

China — electrical machinery, data processing equipment,

Germany —  motor vehicles, machinery, chemicals, textiles, transport equipment, food items,

USA — industrial supplies and materials, food,

Japan — motor vehicles,  semiconductors,

France — agricultural products,  machinery, vehicles,

South Korea — semiconductors, telecommunication equipment,

Netherlands — machinery and equipment, chemicals, fuels,

Italy —  textiles and clothing, production machinery,

Russia — petroleum and other petroleum products,

United Kingdom — manufactured goods, chemicals, food,

 clothing, textiles, iron, steel,  optical and medical equipment.

computer and electronic products,  electrical equipment, pharmaceuticals, metals.
rubber and plastic products,

 automobiles, consumer products,  animal feed, drinks,
fuel and petroleum products, and aircraft.

iron and steel,  auto parts, plastic materials and power generating machinery.

aircraft, 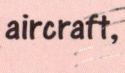 plastics, chemicals,  pharmaceuticals, iron, steel,
 drinks, and electronics.

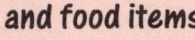 motor vehicles, computers, steel, ships, and petrochemicals.

and food items

 motor vehicles, chemicals, food,  drinks,
engineering products, transport equipment, minerals and nonferrous metals.

natural gas, metals, wood, other wood products, chemicals, military hardware and weapons.

drinks.

World brands

A brand can be a product, a group of products or a company. But it's more than that. It's a name and an association. It's what sticks in your mind when you think of a product or group of products. It is usually a very valuable asset, as people are willing to pay more for products from a company with a strong brand.

World brands

Coca-Cola is probably the brand people around the world recognise most. It means that when you think of a brown, sweet, fizzy drink that makes you feel good, the first words that come into your mind are Coca-Cola. Nike is another brand name that is instantly recognisable.

But a brand is also a promise. Almost every owner of a famous brand has tried hard to establish a set of values that consumers will like and understand. Owners want their brand to represent something trustworthy and honest.

Coca-Cola is a universal drink.

Nike has shops that sell its gear worldwide.

T★p brands?

Each year people are questioned about what they think are the best brands. Interestingly, most high-profile brands began life in the United Sates. You probably recognise all of these:

Gap	Apple
Disney	Nike
McDonalds	Coca-Cola
KFC	Starbucks

Customs

In today's high tech world of international trade, most buying and selling of goods between countries is carried out over the phone, over the Internet or through a bank using a bill of exchange.

Bill of exchange

If a bill of exchange is used, one trader decides what amount must be sent to another trader, then orders their bank to pay it. The bill of exchange shows the amount required, the currency in which it is to be paid, and the date by which it has to be paid.

Taxes and tariffs

Once they've landed at the dock or airport, the goods are taken to a warehouse and stored until they've passed customs inspection.

What is this? Well, governments can make money from international trade. They do this by imposing duty, called a tariff or customs tax, on goods that enter their country.

Believe it or not, tariffs can also be used as a kind of weapon against another country. If country 'A' wants to damage country 'B' for some reason, it can apply such huge customs taxes, that country 'B' can no longer sell at a reasonable price, and its export trade suffers.

WHAT TO PAY

Customs tax
Customs officers are employed to check goods coming in and apply the correct tariff. There are two main types of tariff.

Specific tariffs are where a quantity of an item, such as a barrel of oil, is taxed regardless of its value.

An **"ad valorem"** tariff applies when a tax is calculated as a percentage of the assessed value of an item.

PAYING DUTY

Every time you travel abroad – and when you return home – you will pass through customs. You may even be stopped and checked!

Customs officers check your luggage to make sure there's nothing in it that you need to pay customs duty, or tax, on. You're always allowed a certain amount of stuff tax-free. But you may have to pay tax on items like cameras, watches and so on.

It's best to declare what you have to pay duty on. Not declaring it is an offence, and the penalty will cost you a lot more.

Setting the price

The price of anything is set by two things: the money it has cost to make it and the price people will pay to own it. Some products are what is known as 'price sensitive'. These are goods that are necessities, like toothpaste, which people need but don't put a high value on. Others, are luxuries where price often has nothing to do with cost.

Supply and demand

Supply and demand describes the way a market works – how people decide the amount of a product that they are willing to buy.

If supply and demand are balanced, the number of people who want to buy will equal the amount of a product available to sell.

Overload!

However, if too many people want supplies and these are limited or difficult to get hold of, then problems arise. The price may go up because the product is scarce. If the cost is too high, the demand of buyers will fall. Then, the seller will lose business and maybe fail.

The Right Price

So, it's important to set the price correctly – to make sure it's the price people will pay to own it. The value of anything is the value someone is prepared to pay for it. But most items have a market value too. This is based on what people have generally been prepared to pay for a similar item.

Price is always important. People have a limited amount of money to spend, and if they spend more on one thing, they cannot spend it on another. When the price of a product goes up, other competitive and cheaper products will sell better.

Haggling

Haggling is a way of getting the price reduced, and it's something everyone does. Of course, world traders don't 'haggle', but they do negotiate. Everyone wants to pay the best price, so this often means putting in an offer which the seller can consider.

The seller may want a little more, the buyer offers a little more – slowly the price is established somewhere in the middle, and everyone should be happy.

Gold

Gold is a precious metal. It is valued for its softness, and its ductility, which means it can be drawn easily into fine wires without breaking. It's also very heavy. It weighs nineteen times as much as an equal volume of water. When most metals are heated they start to soften. But gold doesn't absorb heat easily, and therefore it holds its shape even when it's very hot.

Carat gold

Gold is measured in carats. This name came from an old measure that was the same as the weight of a carat, or carob seed.

Gold is a heavy metal.

Carat is now used to judge how pure the gold is. 24 carat gold is the purest kind of gold.

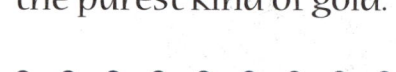

Gold standard

For thousands of years, gold was the standard of value; a base against which to measure currency. This helped countries trade with each other. A country was on the gold standard when it could convert its money into gold if required, and when it agreed to buy or sell gold at a fixed price. By 1900, all leading countries were using the gold standard to trade with each other.

34

Gold Reserves

Nowadays, money is based on the value of the American dollar, and not on the stocks of valuable gold bullion stored around the world. It is still a very valuable metal, but the enormous hoards of gold gathered by governments when gold was the most important measure, now lie in storage.

Today, gold is worth only about one quarter of what it was when its price peaked in 1980. And as the price of gold declines, governments are rethinking their stockpiles. The central banks of the UK, Switzerland, the Netherlands, Belgium, Canada, Argentina and Australia, have all sold significant stocks of gold. Even major gold producers like Australia and Canada are selling.

The Mitsubishi gold bar.

Who's Storing What?

The largest gold reserves are held by the United States Treasury – approximately seven and a half million kilograms of gold is being stored.

The biggest gold bar, weighing 200 kilograms, was made by the Japanese company Mitsubishi Materials Corporation in December 1999. The gold is 99.99 percent pure. The bar measures 19.5 centimetres wide and 40.5 centimetres long at the base, and is 16 centimetres tall.

Bank to bank

Over the years, banks have played a large part in the spread of trade and industry around the world by making money available to merchants, manufacturers and other institutions. Without their contribution, the world might well be a very different place.

How banks started

Unfortunately for the early merchants, the world was not as safe a place as it is today. If they carried a load of money with them, they were in danger of being robbed.

But then, in northern Italy, a few noble families set up banks with agents in different cities. This allowed the merchants to deposit money in their home city in return for a letter of credit. The letter of credit could then be carried on their travels and exchanged for actual money in another place.

Another problem the merchants had was raising the huge sums of money needed to fit out ships as well as buy the goods to trade. Rather than use their own money, they got the banks to lend them the money for a share of the profit.

Bank investors

Today, many large banks have branches all over the world. They trade huge sums of money, investing in foreign currencies, in smaller businesses and large corporations.

The financial centre of Shanghai, China, has an impressive collection of towering banks and finance houses.

Banking is big

Every city in the world now has a banking centre where companies carry out financial business. Some centres are larger and more influential than others, but banking is an important part of the business life of every country. Bankers take decisions that move huge sums of money around the world every second.

The World Bank

The World Bank is not a 'bank' in the real sense of the word. It's one of the agencies of the United Nations, and 184 different countries support it. These countries work together to make sure the Bank has money, and they also control how that money is spent. Together they have set up the World Bank to make sure that the poorer countries of the world get help when they need it.

Free of Poverty

The mission of the World Bank states, 'Our dream is a world free of poverty'. We live in a world where the average person in some countries is very rich, earning more than $40,000 a year. At the same time, the average person in some of the poorest countries only earns $700 a year. There is an enormous gap between these two figures. The poorest people on the planet not only suffer from food shortages, but they miss out on education, on health treatment, on water and electricity – on the basic necessities of life.

To the Rescue

In response, the World Bank helps with loans and grants and with skilled people. The 40 richest countries give billions of dollars each year to be spent on schemes to help people in the poorest 26 countries, to change their lives for the better.

At any one time, the Bank may have up to 2,000 projects in hand, and there are always new emergencies to meet. It sponsors many local projects, such as the installation of much-needed wells and water systems.

A new well brings fresh water to a village.

Orphan children are fed and educated at school.

New schools bring education to everyone.

Goods are despatched from a charity's warehouse.

IMF

IMF stands for **International Monetary Fund**, and while this is also not strictly a bank, it is an organisation that collects and distributes huge sums of money. It has funds of $121 billion – no mean amount!

But who does it lend this money to and why? Like the World Bank, the IMF is dedicated to helping countries around the world, but its work covers all countries, whether rich or poor. It wants to get everyone working and trading together for the benefit of all. If countries co-operate to trade with each other and grow their trade, the world will be more confident and stable.

The IMF aims:

✻ To promote international monetary and exchange stability.
✻ To help expand balanced growth of international trade.
✻ To help establish an easier system of payments between countries.

Sharing money

A group of countries that co-operate and trade with each other, even to the point of sharing the same money, includes 19 of the countries in the European Union. They call themselves the Eurozone.

ECB

The European Central Bank, or ECB as it's known, is the central bank for Europe's single currency the euro.

The euro is a new currency. It was introduced in 1999 in 12 separate countries of Europe, doing away with the franc and lira and Deutschmark and many others. Other countries have now joined.

The ECB's main task is to make sure that the euro is stable, which means watching prices everywhere to make sure one euro buys about the same amount of goods wherever it is used. So, if a cup of coffee costs 1 euro in France, it should be about the same price everywhere else too.

Sharing the euro

Nineteen countries share the Euro:
* Austria
* Belgium
* Cyprus
* Estonia
* Finland
* France
* Germany
* Greece
* Ireland
* Italy
* Latvia
* Luxembourg
* Malta
* Netherlands
* Portugal
* Slovenia
* Slovakia
* Spain
* Lithuania

A single currency

What does it mean to share your money with other countries, most of whom speak a different language, are thousands of kilometres away, and who live their lives and go about their work in a different way too?

It has proved a lot more difficult and a lot less successful than many thought back in 1999.

The smart, new headquarters of the European Bank under construction.

Does Euro-sharing work?

Yes

✳ Trade is made much easier because it removes the need to exchange money.
✳ The risk of different currencies losing value is removed.
✳ A citizen of Europe can find the best price for a product from any Euro country.
✳ Labour and goods can flow more easily between countries.
✳ Money is managed by the ECB so is not influenced by a specific government.

No

✳ The system is more in favour of the larger euro countries than the smaller ones.
✳ If countries get into too much debt they can cause problems for other countries in the system.
✳ A strong euro can make goods more expensive to buy and so threaten exports.

World wealth

As well as rich people, there are also rich countries. These usually become wealthy because of the trade that they do with other countries, perhaps selling raw materials, such as iron and timber, or even the particular skills of their people.

GDP

The world's richest nations are measured by how much each person living in the country contributes to its overall wealth – or earns – in any year. It's called the Gross Domestic Product or GDP.

The United States is a good example of a country that has vast amounts of natural resources, and has used them to become wealthy. Small countries in the Middle East are rich because they export valuable oil. Luxembourg is small and not industrial, but many rich people live there for tax reasons.

The Richest:

* 1 Qatar
* 2 Luxembourg
* 3 Singapore
* 4 Norway
* 5 Brunei Darussalam
* 6 Hong Kong China
* 7 United States
* 8 UAE
* 9 Switzerland
* 10 Australia
* 11 Canada
* 12 Austria
* 13 Ireland
* 14 Netherlands
* 15 Sweden
* 16 Iceland
* 17 Taiwan China
* 18 Germany
* 19 Kuwait
* 20 Denmark

The USA, Argentina and Australia have large land areas where cattle are reared and exported worldwide as meat.

South Korea has a large shipbuilding industry. It sells its ships worldwide.

Qatar, Brunei, UAE, and Kuwait have oil to export worldwide.

Cost of living

Some countries may be wealthy but they are also very expensive to live in. They have what is known as a high cost of living.

If you want to make money and live cheaply, these are the places to avoid:

* Japan
* South Korea
* Russia
* Taiwan China
* Norway
* Hong Kong China
* Switzerland
* Denmark
* Argentina
* China

G7

The G7 is a term used to describe the seven most advanced business and industrial countries in the world.

Working together

The purpose of the G7 is to discuss, and possibly to influence, economic and political situations in the world through an annual summit meeting as well as various other policy meetings and research gatherings. The location of the meeting changes each year among the member states.

* Canada
* France
* Germany
* Italy
* Japan
* United Kingdom
* United States

Recently, the annual meetings have been the focus of protests against large corporations who are seen as growing too fast (and who are greedy for profits). The member countries are sometimes seen to be more interested in increasing their own wealth than in helping poorer countries increase theirs. However, they do agree on large issues such as world peace, and work together to resolve conflicts.

Rising giants

Perhaps the G7 membership is out of date! New rich countries are emerging. China contributes three times as much to global growth, than all 12 member countries of Europe combined. And India isn't far behind. The world economy is shifting, and the biggest players should be at the table! So now there is a larger organisation consisting of 19 countries plus the European Union.

- Australia
- India
- Argentina
- France
- China
- Canada
- Russia
- Brazil
- Germany
- Indonesia
- Saudi Arabia
- South Africa
- Mexico
- Italy
- Japan
- United States
- Turkey
- United Kingdom
- South Korea
- The European Union

Speeding up

And things continue to change all the time. When richer countries run into problems, their economies can slow down to a standstill – or even worse! (See light blue and pale yellow on the chart below.) Meanwhile, poorer countries – many in Africa, South America and Asia – benefit from investment and money gifts, or aid, and start to grow – fast! (See orange and red on the chart.)

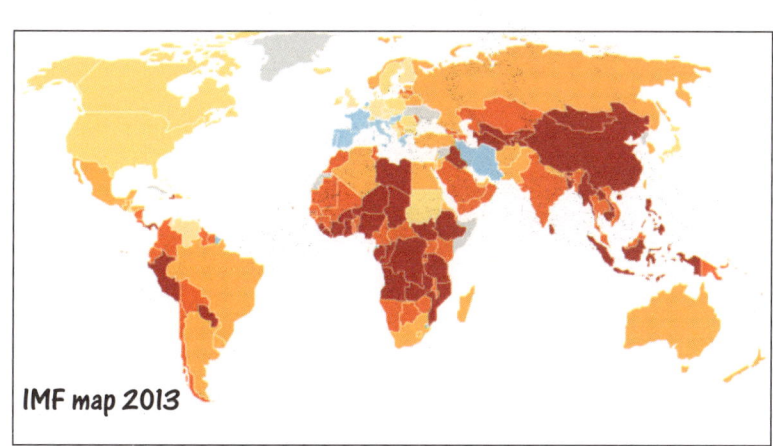

IMF map 2013

World poverty

Just like people, whole countries can be considered poor. A poor country is one that has a low GDP per person, one that has few natural resources, or one that doesn't export many goods to make money. The reasons behind the poverty can be put down to natural causes, such as the weather, soil makeup or geography. It's difficult to grow enough to feed the population or sell abroad if the land is desert. Or perhaps there aren't any rich minerals or metals or oil, to be mined and sold.

Millions in poverty

Poverty means not being able to contribute to the society in which you live. It means suffering shortages, illiteracy and poor health. It means living in areas that take the brunt of environmental damage, such as busy, congested roads, factories, and even waste dumps. You may even need to use the dump to find food, or objects to sell for a living!

And it means living with little self-respect or hope for the future. Around a billion of the world's people live in these desperate conditions.

The Poorest

* Haiti
* Nepal
* South Sudan
* Comoros
* Guinea-Bissau
* Mozambique
* Ethiopia
* Guinea
* Togo
* Mali
* Afghanistan
* Madagascar
* Malawi
* Niger
* Central African Republic
* Eritrea
* Liberia
* Burundi
* Zimbabwe
* Congo - Kinshasa

Why Poor?

There are many reasons why some countries are poor. Climate may play a part. Often, both climate conditions and unexpected natural disasters contribute to poverty. Some cities hold too many people, and many cannot find work or a home.

Homes made of scraps are put together on wasteland.

Slums such as these breed disease and sickness.

No Resources

There may be few natural resources a country can use to either develop its own economy or to sell abroad as exports. Or it may not have easy access to foreign markets. In many poor countries, there's no history of modern industry, the kind that has created wealth for the industrialised countries of the world. Also, some of the poor countries have been dependent on commodities that have dropped in value.

1.2 billion people on our planet are trying to live on less than a dollar a day.

Evening things out

One thing that has not helped the poor countries is debt. Many of them have borrowed money from rich countries over the years to help feed their people – even to help pay for their wars.

3rd World Debt

We all know what it means to have a personal debt we can't repay – even if it's just to our mum! But what if it's a country that's borrowed the money and can't pay back the debt?

At the beginning of the year 2000, the World Bank had listed 42 countries as being in debt. These countries are sometimes called HIPCs, which means Heavily Indebted Poor Countries. Many had debts that were so great that they could not pay all the interest on them – let alone pay back the debt itself.

And to make matters worse, debt repayment was using up the money that could be better spent on health, education and building.

Cancelling Debts

Something had to be done, and in 1996, everyone finally agreed that poor countries needed to get rid of their debt burdens, and that these should simply be written off and forgotten.

No Debt Successes

To qualify to have debts cancelled, the countries had to use the money they would have used to repay their debts on programmes that would get rid of hunger and poverty instead.

Today, 32 of the 40 countries listed have worked with the World Bank and IMF to achieve this, and have had their debts cancelled,

Aid helps

Some countries have been even more successful. The top ten fastest growing countries in the world have included Angola, Myanmar, Ethiopia, Cambodia, Nigeria and Rwanda – all currently large aid recipients. The World Bank blog states that most of today's stable low-income countries will reach middle-income status by 2025.

A small amount of cash helps farmers plant and harvest surplus crops for sale.

Give knowledge

Maybe there will never be loans to poor countries again. Now it is accepted that helping with knowledge, education and skills training is probably more useful than cash.

Fair trade

For many years, the richer countries have produced more food than they need. But rather than tell their farmers to produce less, they have insisted that the poorer countries take their **surplus** mountains of sugar, wheat, rice and so on – at bargain prices.

Handouts

Now this sounds as if it might be helpful. But of course, it hasn't been helpful at all! The imported food was priced cheaper than the local produce. So while the rich country farmers were getting rid of their surplus stock – AND getting paid for it – the farmers in the poorer countries were losing business and money!

The symbol of the Fair Trade organisation.

It's not fair!

Large corporations can get away with this. Their wealth gives them great power – enough to influence governments. Of course, this isn't fair.

So, some smaller companies have helped to set up a system called **Fair Trade** where the farmer or other supplier is paid a fair amount for the goods they supply.

Fair and green

Do you think about what you are buying? Are you a 'green shopper'?

Like Fair Trade, green buying takes us back to ethics. It's about purchasing stuff that's healthy or that doesn't consume an entire rainforest in South America. Working together with millions of others, everyone of us can help have a huge impact on the environment. Although we don't always see the effects, everything we buy comes from the Earth and returns to it in one form or another.

Green buying

Green buying isn't always easy because you may have to pay a bit more for your items and because outlets are hard to find. But if you buy stuff that's better for the planet, you will be joining many millions of people who want to make a difference.

Banana growers work together to make Fair Trade agreements with buyers worldwide.

Buy carefully

'Trade Coffee Company' makes sure its coffee farmers aren't underpaid. You can buy their coffee in many stores and some cafes.

'Body Shop' is another company that makes sure that when it buys ingredients for its cosmetics, the supplier is properly paid.

Disaster!

Unfortunately, any country can be hit by some kind of disaster from time to time. This may be a flood, earthquake, even a war. Such disasters quickly have an effect on business and trade – and on a country's ability to function properly.

Drought ...

Unfortunately, no one can do much about a natural disaster until after it's happened. Many parts of northern and central Africa have a history of drought. The only difference is that these droughts are now happening every five years instead of every 10 to 15, and they are more severe than ever. Droughts bring crop failure and hunger to the people.

... and hunger

Other factors contribute to famine as well, including a high population growth rate, smaller farm sizes, poor farming techniques, deforestation and poor soil.

Each year, for example, two billion tonnes of topsoil is either blown away or washed down the Blue Nile to Egypt. This has come from farmland further south, whose farmers depend on it to grow their crops.

Food help

Given the size of the problem, it's easy to see why a natural disaster such as drought can cause terrible suffering. Many countries still depend on food aid to feed millions of their people.

Wars

When a war breaks out, either between countries or between groups within countries, millions of dollars are spent on soldiers and military equipment that could have been used to buy food. It is estimated that millions of dollars a day are spent on fighting wars around the world.

Apart from the pain and terror and upheaval to people's lives, wars take up manpower and resources that could be better used to build a country's economy and raise everyone's standard of living.

Men sent to fight are not serving their country's growth and prosperity.

Refugees from wars must live in makeshift camps.

At war!

Wars are currently being fought in all these countries.

* South Sudan
* Lebanon
* Iraq
* Syria
* Kenya
* Yemen
* Democratic Republic of the Congo
* Philippines
* India
* Afghanistan
* Colombia
* Mali
* Egypt
* Somalia
* Nigeria
* Libya
* Turkey
* Russia
* Ukraine
* Israel
* Sri Lanka
* Uganda
* Burma-Myanmar

Helping each other

It's all too easy to grow up in your own world and close your eyes to what's going on outside. But every headline on TV or in the newspapers is trying to inform you about problems and injustices outside the comfort of your own home. If you care about what goes on in the world and the people who share it with you, and want to be a 'citizen of the planet', then now is the time to take an interest.

Charities

Charities are organisations that give help in many different forms to those in need. There are many large charities you will have heard of – and maybe helped from time to time. These have an excellent reputation for rushing to a disaster zone and bringing immediate relief. They also work over the long-term, to improve education and health wherever they are based.

Young children learn first skills at school.

UNICEF

The United Nations Children's Fund, or **UNICEF**, is a charity that works for children's rights. It sponsors projects to provide a good basic education for all children, both boys and girls. Some countries do not educate girls with the same care. Health projects are also important. UNICEF tries to reach as many children as possible with life-saving vaccines. Exploited or abused children are a priority. Many children are forced into the army or into **child labour**, working long hours for little pay.

Red Cross

The **Red Cross and Red Crescent Movement** is the largest independent humanitarian network in the world, with more than 100 million members. The organisation tries to respond quickly to disasters and conflicts around the world. It offers food, water, shelter and medical supplies, as well as providing training and repairing hospitals. It also advises on issues such as land mine dangers.

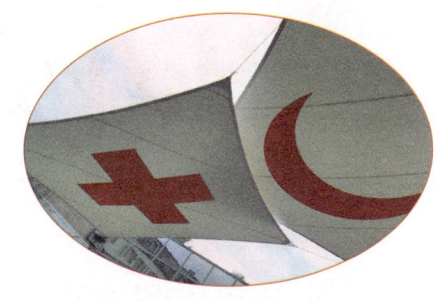

The symbols of the Red Cross and Red Crescent.

Red Cross volunteers assist with food parcels.

Save the Children

Save the Children works in 40 countries around the world. Its aim is to help families improve the health and educational opportunities of their children, as well as to provide money where needed. It is able to organise speedy assistance for children caught in disasters, such as tsunamis, earthquakes and wars.

The charity distributes basic foods such as rice, milk and bread in places like the Sudan. Here, drought conditions have caused malnutrition and other diseases.

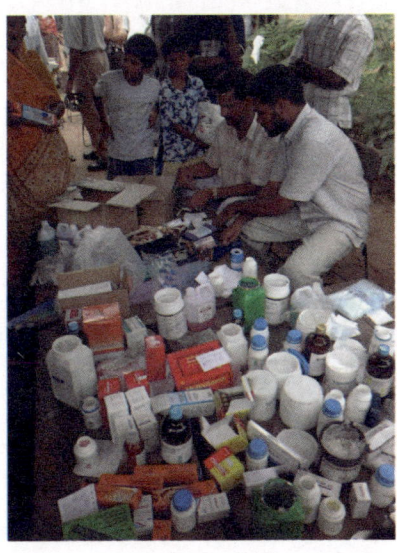

Medical supplied are always needed.

Happy wealth

The World Bank has normally judged the wealth of its 180 member countries around the world by their money wealth. But now it measures things like education provision, human rights records and life-expectancy, as well as cultural values and activities for self-improvement and group participation.

GNH not GDP

In the kingdom of Bhutan, a mountainous country high in the Himalayan mountains, they go even further. Here the ruler, King Jigme Singye Wangchuck, believes that happiness is more important than wealth. Bhutan is the only country in the world to measure its well-being by Gross National Happiness (GNH).

Priority

Most countries worry about their ability to buy and sell things, and whether they can afford all the things they need and want. But not Bhutan! King Wangchuck thinks that if his country tries to develop in line with other countries, it will need to sacrifice its old-fashioned traditions, its heritage and culture, and its beautiful mountain environment. Here in Bhutan, happiness really does take priority over economic wealth.

The Value of a Simple Life

In some religions, happiness is not decided by what we have and own – although this can be useful in reducing poverty and encouraging people to generosity – but by our knowledge, our imagination and our living skills.

A statue of Mohandas Gandhi

Gandhi

Mohandas Gandhi was a Hindu lawyer who helped India become an independent nation. He was a great politician and thinker but he also became a symbol of simple values. He believed that living a simple life would bring more happiness than seeking financial wealth.

So Who is Right?

Should the success of a nation be judged by its ability to produce and consume, or should it be based on the quality of life in that country, the happiness of its people? Should we put more value on things such as fresh water, green forests, clean air, traditional ways of life? If a country makes money from cutting down logs, should it not deduct the loss of the forest from its profits?

United world

Working together

We'd all like to see a stable world where everyone has an opportunity to make the best of their life regardless of what background they come from. Unfortunately, poverty exists everywhere. Hundreds of millions of people live in poverty, even in the richest nations of the world.

It seems incredible that in a world where there's so much wealth and so much money, that anyone should be poor at all. Institutions such as the IMF try to do what they can to create a more balanced world. But it isn't easy.

Can you help?

You may think that in this vast globe of ours most things happen without your being able to influence them. So it's easy to shrug and say there's nothing you can do. But just being aware of what is going on around the world is an important start.

You now know ...

... that contributing to charities helps – especially when there is some disaster, and lives may be changed by even the smallest donation. If you refuse to buy products made with child labour, you might just help to stop this practice. And looking for the Fair Trade sign on food helps traders who need it.

Money isn't everything

You are also now aware that although money is what makes the world tick, there are other things that can and do count and which are just as important.

Glossary

3rd world debt
Money that is owed to rich countries by the poorer countries of the world.

aid
Money, as well as foods, medicines or other supplies, that are often sent to poorer countries who need them.

balance of payments
The difference between the amount of money a country receives from exports, and the amount it spends on imports.

brand
A mark or name on a manufacturer's products which is easily recognised.

charity
An organisation that provides money or help to people who need it.

commodity
The name given to essential products, such as grains and metals, that are bought and sold in large quantities around the world.

currency
The money that is used in a particular country.

debt
Borrowed money to be repaid.

economy
The system of trade and industry by which the wealth of a country is made and used.

export
The sale of goods to other countries overseas.

Fair Trade
A system where buyers and sellers agree a fair and just price for their goods. Fair Trade goods are labelled in the shops.

GDP
This stands for Gross Domestic Product.

government
The group of people elected to run a country on behalf of its people.

import
To buy goods from overseas.

legal tender
The currency of a country in coins and notes that is legally accepted for trade.

market value
The price that something could be sold for at a particular time.

merchant
A person or business that buys and sells products in large amounts for profit, often trading with other countries.

natural resource
Materials such as water, coal, and wood that exist in nature and can be used by people to make other products.

poverty
The state of not having enough money for basic needs.

price
The cost of buying something that usually reflects the cost of making it as well as the price people will pay for it.

specialisation
A special area of production where a country can succeed and export.

supply and demand
The idea that the price of something depends on how much there is available and how many people want to buy it.

tariff
A tax imposed on imported goods and services to restrict trade by increasing the price.

trade gap
A situation in which the value of a country's imports is greater than the value of goods it exports.

Index

3rd world debt 48
ad valorem tax 31
aid 45, 49, 52
amber 12
balance of payments 25
bank 2, 19, 36, 37, 38, 39, 40, 41, 48, 49, 56
banknote 5, 13, 17
barter 6, 7
bead 12
Bhutan 14, 56
bill of exchange 30
brand 28, 60
carat 34
charity 39, 54, 55
child labour 59
climate 21, 47
coin 5, 12, 13, 17
Columbus 8
commodity 21, 47, 60
container ship 11
cost 19, 22, 31, 32, 60, 61

cowrie shell 12
currency 2, 13, 14, 16, 17, 18, 19, 37, 41
customs 30, 31
debt 41, 48, 49, 60
denomination 13
disaster 52, 54, 59
disease 55
dollar 5, 13, 14, 15, 18, 35, 47
drought 52, 55
duty 22, 30, 31
eBay 23
economy 3, 24, 45, 47, 53
education 38, 39, 48, 49, 54, 56
emergency 38
Euro 13, 40
Europe 12, 13, 40, 41, 45
European Union 40
Eurozone 40
export 23

face value 13
Fair Trade 50, 51, 59
financial centre 37
foreign currency 16
G7 44, 45
gold 12
gold reserve 35
gold standard 34
government 4, 13, 41, 60, 61
Gross Domestic Product (GDP) 42, 46
Gross National Happiness 56
haggling 33
Heavily Indebted Poor Countries (HIPC) 48
heritage 56
import 22, 24, 25
industry 36, 43, 47
International Monetary Fund (IMF) 39, 45, 49, 58

62

internet 30
investment 45, 61
labour 41
legal tender 13
letter of credit 36
Magellan 8
malnutrition 55
Marco Polo 8
market 6, 19, 23, 32, 33
market value 33
medium of exchange 7
merchant 8
Mohandas Gandhi 57
natural disaster 47
natural resource 46, 47
negotiate 33
note 5, 7, 12, 13, 16, 17
oil 9, 19, 21, 31, 42, 43, 46
online trading 23
population 46, 52
port 8, 10, 11
pound 14, 15

poverty 3, 38, 46, 47, 49, 57, 58, 61
price 2, 30, 32, 33, 34, 35, 40, 41, 60, 61
product 9, 20, 27, 28, 32, 33, 41, 59, 60, 61
profit 36, 44, 57
purchasing power 5
quota 22
receipt 12
Red Crescent 55
Red Cross 55
refugee 53
Save the Children 55
silver 12
specialisation 20
standard measure 12
supply and demand 32
surplus 6, 49, 50
tariff 30, 31
tax 22, 30, 31, 42, 60, 61
European Central Bank 40
trade balance 24

trade gap 24
trade route 8
UNICEF 54
United Nations 38
unit of value 7
Vasco da Gama 8
war 5, 52, 53
wealth 3, 4, 23, 42, 44, 47, 50, 56, 57, 58
World Bank 38, 39, 48, 49, 56
world peace 44
yuan 14, 16, 18
Zheng He 8

63

绿色印刷　保护环境　爱护健康

亲爱的读者朋友：

本书已入选"北京市绿色印刷工程——优秀出版物绿色印刷示范项目"。它采用绿色印刷标准印制，在封底印有"绿色印刷产品"标志。

按照国家环境标准（HJ2503-2011）《环境标志产品技术要求 印刷 第一部分：平版印刷》，本书选用环保型纸张、油墨、胶水等原辅材料，生产过程注重节能减排，印刷产品符合人体健康要求。

选择绿色印刷图书，畅享环保健康阅读！

北京市绿色印刷工程

图书在版编目（CIP）数据

世界货币：我们这个世界是如何花钱的？为什么要花钱？：汉、英／（英）贝利；（英）劳著；（英）比奇插图；傅瑞蓉译．—北京：华夏出版社，2016.1

（华夏少儿金融智慧屋. 货币系列）

书名原文：World Money : How the World Spends its Money, and Why?

ISBN 978-7-5080-8704-7

Ⅰ.①世… Ⅱ.①贝… ②劳… ③比… ④傅… Ⅲ.①货币—世界—少儿读物—汉、英 Ⅳ.①F821-49

中国版本图书馆 CIP 数据核字（2015）第 306745 号

World Money : How the World Spends its Money, and Why?
Copyright©2014 BrambleKids Ltd
All rights reserved
The simplified Chinese translation rights arranged through Rightol Media（本书中文简体版权经由锐拓传媒取得 Email:copyright@rightol.com）
CHINESE SIMPLIFIED Language adaptation edition published by BrambleKids Ltd., and HUAXIA PUBLISHING HOUSE Copyright © 2016
All Rights Reserved

版权所有　翻版必究
北京市版权局著作权合同登记号：图字 01-2015-2441

世界货币——我们这个世界是如何花钱的？为什么要花钱？

作　　者	［英］格里·贝利　　［英］费利西娅·劳
插　　图	［英］马克·比奇
译　　者	傅瑞蓉
责任编辑	李雪飞
出版发行	华夏出版社
经　　销	新华书店
印　　装	北京中科印刷有限公司
版　　次	2016 年 1 月北京第 1 版　　2016 年 1 月北京第 1 次印刷
开　　本	787×1030　1/16
印　　张	8
字　　数	140 千字
定　　价	39.80 元

华夏出版社　地址：北京市东直门外香河园北里 4 号　邮编：100028
网址：www.hxph.com.cn　电话：（010）64663331（转）
若发现本版图书有印装质量问题，请与我社营销中心联系调换。